Sir William Martin Conway

Early Flemish Artists and their Predecessors on the Lower Rhine

Sir William Martin Conway

Early Flemish Artists and their Predecessors on the Lower Rhine

ISBN/EAN: 9783337366247

Printed in Europe, USA, Canada, Australia, Japan

Cover: Foto ©Thomas Meinert / pixelio.de

More available books at **www.hansebooks.com**

EARLY
FLEMISH ARTISTS

*AND THEIR PREDECESSORS ON
THE* Lower Rhine

BY

WILLIAM MARTIN CONWAY

Roscoe Professor of Art, University College, Liverpool
Author of
"The Artistic Development of Reynolds and Gainsborough,"
"Woodcutters of the Netherlands," etc.

With Twenty-nine Illustrations

LONDON
SEELEY & CO., 46, 47, & 48, ESSEX STREET, STRAND

1887

CONTENTS.

CHAPTER VII.

CHAPTER VIII.

CHAPTER IX.

LIST OF ILLUSTRATIONS.

EARLY FLEMISH ARTISTS.

CHAPTER I.

THE RISE OF PAINTING IN THE NORTH.

CONSIDERING the attention bestowed for centuries upon the history, literature, and arts of Greece, it is not surprising that the study of Greek civilization as a united whole should have advanced further than that of the civilization of any other epoch. Greek literature is of moderate length and wide compass. Greek history is enshrined in it, and in the memorials of Greek art, themselves relatively speaking few in number. Thus the studies of these three main factors of Greek civilization have naturally gone forward hand in hand. So also has it been with the investigations more recently set on foot to win back some knowledge of the buried and forgotten civilizations of Assyria and Egypt. Historical students are

B

forced by the dearth of other materials to consider the memorials of ancient art with fullest attention. It has however been different with the Middle Ages. They lie too near us. Influences from them still recognizably affect our lives. Our knowledge of the general sequence of events in them, drawn from contemporary records and chronicles, is tolerably complete. Their most obvious importance to us lies in the direct descent from them of our political institutions. Thus the study of mediæval history is one-sided. Minute investigation has been lavished upon certain aspects of the mediæval past, whilst other aspects, of equal importance, have received slight attention. Of the rise, culmination, decline, and after-effect of Greek or Roman civilization every educated person has some sort of general idea ; but relatively few comprehend, in their backward glance over the history of Europe, any similar understanding of the epochs of growth and decay through which its various peoples have passed. In coming years a change will take place in this matter. Already the Dark Ages are being touched by the dawn of a renewed existence. The day of their after-life is at hand.

The people of the seventeenth and eighteenth centuries, in their scorn, gave the name of Dark to all that period which intervened between the fall of the Roman Empire and the beginning of the so-called

Renascence, thereby declaring plainly enough that that period was one from which they were wholly cut off in sympathy and the general tone and aims of life. It was in fact a world-epoch altogether different from the one in which we live ; and a world-epoch is not a mere scale of succeeding events, but a great symphony of existence, played on the throbbing lives of men. It has to be regarded as a whole, as the working out of a noble theme, any one-sided investigation of which will lead only to a one-sided result. The politician may learn lessons from it for the guidance of his policy ; the economist may use it as a test for his theories ; the artist may draw examples from it, and the man of letters may find certain of its written works suggestive to him ; but one whose interest in the world is based upon the full breadth of his manhood, must turn back and view it as a whole from every side. Regarded thus the Dark or Gothic period must in future times come to rank among the greatest epochs. Do you ask for heroisms, and will the age of St. Louis of France and St. Francis of Assisi send you unsatisfied away ? Do you demand great thoughts, and shall you not find them in a Bernard of Clairvaux or a Thomas Aquinas ? Must you have beauty of utterance, and will not the songs of a Walter von der Vogelweide or the almost Homeric Chanson de Roland more than satisfy your need ? Is it splendour of art you

B 2

require? Enter beneath the sculptured portal of Our
Lady of Paris, and say, have any people (even the
Greeks themselves) attained higher rank in the
expression of noble thought through the language of
the chisel? Has the brush of the painter been more
deftly wielded than by the tender hand of a Wilhelm
of Köln? Have ever stones been more gloriously
builded together than by the thirteenth-century
architects of the Ile de France? Have walls ever
glowed with a finer iridescence of colour than the
Gothic painters shed over them in their joy? Have
richer hangings been woven, more tasteful costumes
been designed, more expressive ceremonials acted,
more beautiful domestic adornments made, in the
shape of furniture, jewellery, illuminated volumes, and
other articles of use, than by the men of the Gothic
age? Where will you find a grander conception of
the governance of mankind than in the mediæval
idea of a world-Emperor and a world-Bishop?
Where will you find a nobler knitting together of
man and man than in the feudal system and the
guilds? Where will you look for greater enterprises
than in the age of the Crusades, or more devoted self-
sacrifice than in the cells of many and many a scarce-
remembered monk? Where, throughout all the ages
and races of humanity, will you discover a more
divine ideal of the invisible and eternal world than
that which in the Middle Ages was not alone the

faith of the poet and the scholar, but the satisfaction of the labourer and the craftsman too?

One spirit animated the whole of this mediæval civilization, and expressed itself in various ways. Political history does not reveal it except in part. It is only by entering into the life of the folk, reading the books of their great men, looking at the works of their artists, considering what it was towards which they aimed, and what it was they most universally admired, that the modern mind can be brought in contact with the mediæval spirit. It will not be uninteresting, therefore, to consider briefly the general tone and tendency of the paintings made by northern artists during the Middle Ages, with a view, if possible, to discover what manner of thing the people of those days loved to imagine and to see depicted for them—what, in fact, was their ideal.

The materials for this consideration are tolerably numerous, but, unfortunately, very inaccessible. Old writers, old account-books and other archives, lead us to the conclusion that in the thirteenth and four-teenth centuries the walls of every important building were all glorious with fine colours within, and some-times also without. It was customary not alone to paint figures, or at any rate decorative patterns, upon the surface of a wall or a roof, but also to colour and gild the mouldings and the statuary with which

portals and other parts of an edifice were usually
adorned. These mural decorations were painted in
distemper upon a fine coating of plaster, and of
course rapidly yielded to the action of the weather.
For this reason, if for no other, we should naturally
expect but few specimens of such work to remain.
Add the common habit in the seventeenth and
eighteenth centuries of whitewashing over any Gothic
painted works which had survived ; add the still
more pernicious restoration craze which destroyed
in cold blood a great part of the few remaining
fragments, and the rarity of mediæval wall-paintings
in the north of Europe is sufficiently explained.
Though rare, however, they can be found, and enough
of them exist to enable the formation of a sound
estimate of the nature of our loss. In England there
are plenty, notwithstanding the enmity of an un-
generous Protestantism. In the Low Countries there
are not a few. Germany and France are somewhat
richer. Such paintings, however, must be sought out,
and the student will have to travel from city to city,
and from village to village, finding here the remains
of a figure, there the traces of a decorative pattern,
and only now and then any tolerably preserved
composition worthy the name of a picture. Moreover, such works do not appeal to any but a very
small section of the public, and so the photographer
remains ignorant of them, or passes them by with

scorn as he sets up his camera before some newly-
erected statue of a worthy whose name will be
forgotten a century hence. For the purposes, therefore, of the ordinary student wall-paintings are relatively little important. Their place is excellently
supplied by stained glass windows, whereof a larger
quantity remain, and by illuminated manuscripts,
which may be seen and studied in all the principal
libraries of Europe.

A comparison of pictures upon walls and glass with
those in MSS. shows conclusively that the same
general style of work prevailed in all three, allowance
being made for the different treatments rendered
necessary by different conditions. Indeed for all
artists of any one time and period there must be one
ideal shared by them in common with the men for
whom they work. Now if the ideal of the Gothic
artists could be put into few words, we should not
have to pause long over this matter. But the statement of that ideal employed the combined labours
of thousands of painters, sculptors, preachers, poets,
and philosophers, and a modern writer may well
pause before attempting to do alone in a chapter
what employed such a company for two centuries.
It is only by coming directly in contact with the
works of mediæval art that one can be oneself
imbued with a knowledge of the mediæval spirit.

A great Gothic building cannot be understood at a

glance. The mass of it, the balance and building of
it, do indeed produce an immediate general effect
upon the spectator, but it is in the details of ornament
that the voice of the edifice is to be heard. Travellers
too often content themselves with a hasty passage up
the nave and down the aisles of some great cathedral ;
perhaps they glance at the treasury, and sometimes
they even walk once round the exterior. Then they
think they have seen all there is to see, and they move
on to look at something else. Upon the few who go
more intelligently to work, and for whom details are
things of a certain moment, the grotesque parts of
the sculptured ornament not uncommonly leave the
strongest impression. They think of these Gothic-
minded folk as a humorous set, and perhaps as men
of little reverence, the notion of illustrating one's
prayer-book with comic designs being rather out of
keeping with present ideas. The great mediæval
cathedrals were prayer-books graven in stone. They
symbolized and expressed all that the mediæval man
believed of the world that is, was, and is to come. In
that day of harmony between religion and daily life
there was no distinction of kind between week-day
and Sunday, or between the adornment of a house
and that of a church. Household implements were
embellished with carvings of sacred subjects as
naturally as the furniture of a cathedral ; and con-
versely it seemed just as natural to sculpture incidents

of every-day life in a church portal as images of the
most sacred personages of Bible history. The Reformation was the great wedge which sundered religion
from daily life. Before it the two were merely different
aspects of the same thing. Now exactly the kind of
subjects that a mediæval mason sculptured upon
churches, houses, municipal buildings, and everywhere
else where his assistance was called for, mediæval
painters likewise painted and mediæval miniaturists
illuminated. The ideal for all of them was the same,
and you can find that ideal informed just as well in
carved ivories, pieces of goldsmith's or ironsmith's
work, carved wooden implements, or woven stuffs, as in
sculptured portals or illuminated volumes. In attempting, therefore, to form some notion of the ideal of the
Gothic painter, we may draw illustrations indiscriminately from works of art of whatever kind. The same
set of subjects and the same kind of treatment (in so
far as the materials used permit of it) are everywhere
to be found, because the same ideal is everywhere
striving for expression.

Now, as has been said, it is the grotesque element
in mediæval art which usually makes the strongest
impression upon the modern student, and we may
therefore consider that element first. In doing so,
however, we must at the outset guard ourselves from
the wholly false assumption that Gothic art was
mainly an art of humour. It is only because in that

respect we are out of harmony with these old artists that the grotesque element of their work strikes us so powerfully. It is strange to us, and therefore we notice it. We have our *Punch* in these days, but it is a separate publication ; we do not mix it up with sermons. Except in the services of the Salvation Army, we are not accustomed to mingle together the comic and the religious. But mediæval art, being a part of mediæval religion, and that being a reflection of every side of life, was ready to express in rapid succession all the various moods and humours of men. Just as the Church had its folk festivals and its solemn religious ceremonies, following one on the heels of another in the same building, and alike under saintly and angelic patronage, art changed from grave to gay, conscious that the eyes which regard mankind from Eternity's stillness look with equal favour upon hours of merriment and hours of worship, and find as great satisfaction in the labour of a man's hands as in the longings of his puzzled heart. The life of Christ, to the Gothic mind, was a permeating influence in the whole course of human life. The husbandman at his plough and the churchman at his prayers were alike fulfilling their heaven-appointed task, and were alike performing a religious action. For this reason you will find that the Gothic church bears always in prominent position representations of the occupations of the months of the year, these occupations being as much a part of the Christian religion as the events of the life of Christ Himself.

In the cathedral of Chartres it is easiest to catch some echo of the voice of a great mediæval church, of the things about which it spoke and the manner of its speaking. That cathedral is remarkable as possessing in tolerable condition three fine sculptured porches by which entry is made from the north, west, and south. It is impossible here to enumerate all the subjects sculptured upon these porches, but the North Porch may be taken as typical of the rest. It speaks chiefly of the Virgin and of her sweet influence, which, to the Gothic mind, embraced all the thoughts and actions of men and angels in the visible and invisible worlds. This porch contains three doorways, each of which is filled above and on either side with sculpture, and in front of all three is a richly-wrought colonnade. In all there are more than 700 carved figures, large and small, many of the highest order of beauty.

The central figure is a colossal statue of St. Anne holding the Virgin in her arms, and standing on a bracket carved with the story of Joachim. Overhead the chief subjects are the Death, Assumption, and Coronation of the Virgin. Three incidents from the birth and early days of the infant Jesus are carved over the door on the left, their object being to tell the great central fact of the Virgin's life, whilst in a

corresponding position on the right are the Judgment
of Solomon and the Sufferings of Job—events typical
of Justice and patient Endurance, the leading virtues
of the Virgin herself. The setting for these jewels is
of an astonishing richness, every subject hereafter
mentioned being introduced into the position it holds
with intent to suggest side-lights of thought, each
being connected with its neighbours above and below
and contrasted with those that balance it in corresponding positions. There are forty-two colossal
statues, twenty-six being of Saints and Prophets, two
representing the Annunciation, two the Visitation, two
the symbolical figures of the Synagogue and the.
Church, or the Old and New Dispensation, two the
symbolical figures of the Active and Contemplative
Life, and the remaining eight being intended for
portraits of the royal and noble personages by whose
munificence or under whose rule this great work of art
was made. These forty-two persons stand upon
brackets richly carved with subjects illustrative of
their lives. Around the arched-over part of each
door come rows of angels, some of them representing
the sun, moon, and stars ; then there are the physical
and spiritual ancestors of the Virgin, and a number
of representatives of the human race, engaged in
adoration of the Lady of Pity. To these succeed
series of carvings depicting the chief incidents in the
lives of Samson and Gideon, Esther and Judith,

Tobit, David and Samuel,—each of whom was regarded as a type of one side or other of the ideal
character. Further, we have the whole story of the
Creation, the Fall, and the condemnation of man
to a life of labour and sorrow. We are thus led
to consider the various occupations of the months,
accompanied by the signs of the zodiac and figures
emblematic of Summer and Winter. Next come the
arts and sciences; then the various modes of life,
active and contemplative; then, as warning and example, the ten Virgins of the parable, the twelve Fruits
of the Holy Spirit, the fourteen Beatitudes of body
and soul, and the seven Virtues conquering the seven
Vices. The whole is surmounted by a seated figure
of God Most High in the attitude of Benediction.

However strange and difficult to understand all
this sculpture may now be, it is clear at any rate that
it was the work of men not barren in ideas. The
Coronation of the Virgin is the central subject, and
about that the mediæval mind grouped together into
a living unity its conceptions of the duties and joys
of life, its picture of the past and its hopes and fears
of the future. At no time in the world's history did
faith and life march together in such close com-
panionship. The whole of knowledge and all the
acts and events of life formed together part of one
system, and were animated by one faith and subor-
dinated to it. Religion directed and explained every-

thing to the perfect satisfaction of all men. Thus the
artist was gifted with a perfect language. He had
a symbol for every thought ; he could give visible
form to ideas which we can no longer express without the aid of language hard to be understood.

But thus far we have noticed only the North Porch
of Chartres ; the same cathedral possesses two other
porches, one quite and the other almost as rich in
sculpture as this. Moreover, all these sculptures were
once painted and gilt, and the colours were treated
symbolically, and gave further expression to the
artist's thought. Then again these porches were but
the entrances ; the church within was more vocal
even than they. Its walls no doubt were covered
over with paintings, though none of them remain ;
its windows at any rate were filled with storied glass
fortunately in perfect preservation, and forming the
richest store-house of mediæval fancy anywhere in
the world. Corresponding to the three porches are
three great rose windows, representing respectively
the Last Judgment, the Glory of Christ, and the Glory
of the Virgin. In addition to these there are one
hundred and twenty-five double-light windows, thirty-
five smaller rose windows, and twelve little roses, and
almost the whole of this gorgeous jewellery of pictured
thought dates from the thirteenth century. The windows were, for the most part, paid for and presented
to the church by the guilds of workmen of the town ;

many of them, therefore, contain panels representing
the occupations of the trades, subjects drawn with
perfect veracity and perfect art from the folk-life of
the day. Others were presented by royal and noble
personages, who, after the praiseworthy fashion of the
time, had their own portraits introduced into the
work ; in one case the donor and his wife are depicted
playing chess. The subjects of this multitude of trans-
lucent pictures are of the usual kind. The chief incidents in the lives of Christ and the Virgin are to be
found, as well as those of the lives of some fifty saints.
The Apostles, the nine orders of angelic hierarchies,
the patriarchs and prophets of the Old Testament, the
parables of the Prodigal Son, the Good Samaritan,
and the Ten Virgins, are all duly illustrated ; and
besides there are representations of certain less
common subjects, such as the Virgin holding in her
lap the seven Gifts of the Spirit. One window bears
a series of types and antitypes from the Old and New
Testament, another has once again the signs of the
zodiac and the occupations of the months, and a
certain number are occupied by very finely orna-
mented panels of decorative work in *grisaille.*

Such then was the range of subject at the disposal
of the Gothic artist. He had a long series of events
in the sacred history, an almost endless catalogue of
noble deeds, miracles, and heroic sufferings of saints,
and a large number of symbolic and emblematic

figures representing the modes of life, the virtues, vices, gifts of the Spirit, works of mercy, blessings of the soul, and so forth, upon which to exercise his fancy. The great difference between him and the modern artist lay, however, not so much in the choice of subject (for though subjects may be very different, they can be treated in the same spirit), as in the state of mind in which he attacked his work. The modern artist feels that he has to paint a religious picture if possible in a religious frame of mind, a historical subject in an antiquarian frame of mind, a humorous subject in a comic frame of mind, a tragic subject in a tragic frame of mind. The mediæval artist felt no such thing. He went to work on all subjects alike in the frame of mind most natural to himself. He believed so implicitly in everything he undertook to represent, that he never thought he had to make it look creditable. He cared only to make it look pretty. He knew that people would recognize at once the subject of his work, if they looked at it in detail at all, because he was never called upon to depict any except a well-known round of subjects. Every one knew that a female figure holding a lamp upside down was one of the Foolish Virgins, and every one knew that a man with a gridiron was St. Laurence, and they knew all about the Ten Virgins and all about St. Laurence ; there was no call upon the artist to do more than jog their memories. So he had plenty of time for his own little whims and fancies. If he felt merry he showed it in his work, even though that were a picture of some martyrdom. Hence arose the extraordinary and fascinating frequency of grotesque in mediæval times. It invaded the ceremonies, as it did the art, of the Church, and is the quality which most visibly hedges off the feelings of the thirteenth and fourteenth centuries, from our perfect sympathy.

Of course a joke in stone is rather a laborious affair; the Gothic masons could not, therefore, be often openly humorous. Now and again in some little out-of-the-way corner, some spandril of a wall arcading, some knob or corbel, they found a chance to sculpture a grinning little fiend, or a monk-headed, dog-bodied beast, clothed, likely enough, in pontifical attire. But the chief quality of Gothic grotesque is in its slyness. Its creations peep round the corner at you and lurk in secret places, like a monk's joke whispered in church. So if you turn up the underside of a carved seat (one of those known as *misereres*), you will be more certain to find a specimen of this old world humour there than if you walk straight ahead, looking at the objects you cannot help seeing. The Gothic sculptor used grotesque as a reward for the patient observer; moreover, he knew that his fun would lose its flavour if it were continually before the eye in prominent places. So he kept it in reserve,

C

placed it so that it was only seen now and then, as
a relief to those finer and purer thoughts to which
the spectator was more prominently and continually
directed. It must be borne in mind that then people
spent much more of their time in churches than
any one, even the most devout, does now-a-days.
When a man only crosses the threshold of a church
one day in the week after getting himself up, mind
and body, for the occasion, he may find it easy to
be solemn, or even difficult to be anything else. But
the mediæval church was quite a different kind of
place. It was the opera, and the concert-hall, and the
club, and the newspaper, and the place of worship all
joined into one. People went there often, and on
holidays stayed there for a long time; and they did
so because they liked the place, and felt themselves
at home and unconstrained there. They were not
all the time compelled to draw a long face. Perhaps
they had their joke often enough. It is that kind
of spirit, therefore, that Gothic architectural ornament
expresses.

Thirteenth-century painting is merely a part of
architecture. All the arts in the thirteenth century
were but handmaids of architecture. They were
primarily devoted to the adornment of buildings, and
especially religious buildings. Sculpture arose as an
architectural embellishment, and could not help so
arising. Painting was chiefly employed as a com-

pletion for sculpture and as a mural decoration. Other arts not so immediately useful to architecture nevertheless fell under her sway. Carved ivories are always at this time included within an architectural design, embroideries are likewise designed as though the figures on them were sculptured and set in stone niches. If you take up the original binding of some splendid thirteenth-century book, you will find that it is embossed with figures which, reproduced on a larger scale, would be noble works of sculpture. Everywhere the power of the chisel reigned supreme. Miniature painting did not escape the influence. Most thirteenth and fourteenth century illuminated manuscripts were intended for use in the services of the Church. It was not till the fifteenth century that sumptuously adorned chronicles and romances began to be made for the amusement of the wealthy in their hours of leisure. Fine thirteenth-century illuminated MSS. were of two main kinds: either they were Books of Hours, that is to say, the layman's Prayer-Book for private devotions in his own chamber, or else they were service-books to be used in church by the clergy. They were in fact either furniture for the church or for the private oratory. In either case it was but natural that their decoration should be of the same kind as that of all the other ornaments and furniture of the church. A thirteenth-century illu-minated service-book usually contains a number of

C 2

miniatures, of small dimensions, illustrative of the text, and generally connected with borders or ornamental flourishes, splendidly free in design, like the growth of holly or hawthorn. These flourishes are likewise attached to initial letters and present an endless variety. There is never any repetition ; they dart out in one direction or another with absolute crispness and grace, showing the exhaustlessness of the miniaturist's fancy and the trained and governed freedom of his hand. Almost always they are the play-place of grotesques. It was said above that a grotesque carved in stone was rather a laboured joke, one at any rate that had to be set lurking in a secret place. The grotesques in illuminated MSS. were different in that respect. They were drawn on the spur of the moment, and expressed the momentary fancy of the craftsman. Hidden in the pages of a book, they were sufficiently removed from the possibility of wearying the eye by constant visibility. There is thus a freshness and frolicsome humour about these little things, never in the best period descending into license, which makes them unique of their kind, and endows them with a quite pre-eminent and enduring value.

The ordinary miniatures are likewise of great artistic merit. They usually represent events in the sacred history. The manner of treatment is peculiar. The background is almost always a beautiful diaper-

work, against which the figures are relieved, like
painted sculptures before a painted wall. The
number of figures necessary to tell the tale is reduced
to the lowest possible limit ; they are grouped together with great simplicity, and usually in a severely
accurate balance. Each figure is as simple in posture
and clothed in as simple drapery as can be. There
is never an unnecessary line nor a needless fleck of
colour. Details are outlined with a fine pen, and
colours are laid on afterwards simple and pure.
Indeed, purity of line and colour is the leading
characteristic of this Gothic work. There is never
anything elaborate ; all is reserved and direct.
There is no seeking after display. The story is told
in its simplicity, and that is all. The figures, moreover, are all of one type ; men and women possess
one invariable character—invariable except in cases
where brutality or vice has to be depicted, and then
the artists always fail. This uniform character is
the ideal of mediæval legend, song, and tale. It
is the character of man and woman as the makers
of chivalry would have them be. Its leading quality
is purity of heart, absolute stainlessness of soul.
Faces are seldom, perhaps never, intellectual, neither
are they individual ; they possess none of the elements of portrait ; they are repetitions, unfailingly
sweet, of one lovely, all-embracing ideal. It was
this ideal which gave birth to the devotion of monk

and nun, and which sent men in thousands to the
Holy Land to fight the battles of an ideal Lord.   It
was this ideal which raised the peoples of Europe
from the grovelling savagery of the time of the
Invasions, and taught them to be true and generous
and just.   It was this which made possible whatever of manliness and righteous life has been nurtured
in us even to the present day ; an ideal which has
fastened itself as permanently in our thoughts,
let us hope, as in our language, and if it had left
behind it no greater monument than the name of
"gentleman," would in that alone have bequeathed
a richer heritage than many a conquering race in
all its works of pride.

" Unto the pure all things are pure."   Purity, if
it gains a footing in any heart, pervades every action
and leaves a trace in every footprint.   It is not the
only or indeed an absolutely essential virtue ; many
of the great men, many of the great artists, of the
world have lacked it ; but whoever possesses it is
thereby endowed with an irresistible power and a
clearness and unfaltering certainty of insight never
better described than in the great Beatitude, " Blessed
are the pure in heart, for they shall see God."
Painters of the fifteenth and following centuries did
great things, and have left us great monuments of
far-extending power, but in one particular they
seldom equalled their Gothic predecessors.   It was

only Fra Angelico and a few of his immediate companions who were able to give form to ideal creations
in which it is hardly possible to discover a trace of
what we call sin. The Gothic painters seldom failed
in this. Their creations may be lacking in many
of those qualities of strength and intellect which
go to make a rounded human being, but they are
almost always of a spotless purity, fit to be dwellers
in that Divine presence which, to the mediæval
mind, was the essential quality of the heavenly world
to come.

At no time, probably, in the world's history, if we
except the culminating period of Hellenic civilization,
has there reigned a more perfect harmony between
faith and the structure of men's lives than in the
thirteenth century. Holy Catholic Church and Holy
Roman Empire, in theory, at any rate, merely different
aspects of the same world-governance, were reflected
in the two sides of each individual's life. There was
no sunderance of Church and State, no opposition of
science and religion, no splitting into parts of a
man's life or his opinions. The body politic and the
body ecclesiastical were the same thing. Every act
of a man's everyday existence had both its spiritual
and its social aspect. The arts of the central Gothic
epoch give patent evidence of this harmony. They
culminated under the rule of architecture. Painting
was her obedient handmaid. The arts of the glazier,

the weaver, the sculptor were all alike dominated
by the art of the mason.   Goldsmiths, wood-carvers,
workers in ivory, miniaturists, embroiderers, art-
workers of every kind took their forms from those
of the supreme art of the epoch, and combined together to express the same great ideal.

But in the fourteenth century this harmony no
longer existed.   Feudalism was already doomed.
The monastic orders were already corrupt.   The
folk had already begun to resent the pecuniary
exactions of a lazy ecclesiastical order.   The balance
of classes was no longer perfect.   Most ominous of
all, society was no longer united in the acceptance
of a single ideal, dimly or grossly perceived by the
masses, finely by the elect, but substantially the same
for all.   If, in the light of historical experience, we
look back upon the thirteenth century, we can trace
the germs of discord to come ; for every Present
must contain a Future in its womb.   But in the
fourteenth century divisions were latent no longer,
but patent to all.   Society was openly divided into
the two great parties, noble alike—that which clung
to something fine in the past, and that which aimed
at something fine in the future ; Memory animating
the one, Hope the other.

When the Jewish philosophers introduced the
commentaries of Averroës and the Arabians to the
philosophers of Christendom, and thereby gave sub-

stance to the nascent opposition of Nominalist and
Realist, they sowed the seed which was in due time
to produce that convulsed offspring—the Reformation. By the middle of the fourteenth century the
fruit was already formed, though still far from ripe.
The Averroïsts of the thirteenth century, William of
St. Amour and the rest, were succeeded in the fourteenth by Wicklif, in the fifteenth by Huss, and in the
sixteenth by Luther. The Reformation was growing
all those 250 years. In the thirteenth century
religious ideas and ecclesiastical forms of expression
were in harmony together. After the thirteenth
century forms tended towards rigidity and the
Church lost plasticity. It then became certain that
an opposition must sooner or later arise between the
literalists and the spiritualists—the party of strict
adherence to the letter of the Church's custom, and
the party desirous of enlarging the spirit of Christian
doctrine.

For the student of art the fourteenth-century
spiritualists, or "mystics," are a specially interesting
group of men. The Gothic art of a century earlier
had been the art of an entire civilization, similar in
that respect to the arts of ancient Egypt, Assyria,
and Greece. But in the fourteenth century another
state of things prevailed. Local schools began to
show sharp lines of division. Local ideals reigned.
The finest of such local schools was that which

flourished in the Rhine valley under the influence of the mystic preachers.

The fourteenth century was in many respects an awful day in Central Europe. War continually scorched the land; famines followed one another; scarcely was one pestilence past before a worse came in its wake; and when the folk looked to those who should have comforted them with noble hopes, they found them unclean, idle, and mainly concerned with their own temporal welfare. Under such circumstances a small band of men arose, animated with a new and attractive ideal. They demanded not so much splendour of religious ceremonies and frequent observance of religious forms as an inward purification of the heart. Such were Meister Eckhardt (a "profound pantheistic thinker"), Tauler, Suso, and their fellows. They did not sunder themselves from the Church,—the possibility of so doing had not yet occurred to them,—but they protested openly against the evils in the Church, the lewdness and luxury of the clergy, and the growing formalism of the folk. They did not urge their followers to penance, they did not preach good works. They encouraged an enthusiastic yearning of the soul after God, after things unseen and not rationally conceivable, but comprehended by faith. Holiness was the aim of their teaching, and it was to be attained by an entire self-surrender of the soul.

"The mystic," says Mr. Beard,* "is one who claims to be able to see God and Divine things with the inner vision of the soul—a direct apprehension, as the bodily eye apprehends colour, as the bodily ear apprehends sound. His method, as far as he has one, is simply contemplation: he does not argue, or generalize, or infer; he reflects, broods, waits for light. He prepares for Divine communion by a process of self-purification: he detaches his spirit from earthly cares and passions: he studies to be quiet that his still soul may reflect the face of God. He usually sits loose to active duty: for him the felt presence of God dwarfs the world and makes it common: he is so dazzled by the glory of the one great object of contemplation, that he sees and cares for little else. . . . The mystic is always more or less indistinct in utterance: he sees, or thinks he sees, more than he can tell: the realities which he contemplates are too vast, too splendid, too many-sided to be confined within limits of human words. . . . Give a mystic the thought of God, and his mind wants and can contain no more: from a soul so filled, all peculiarities of ecclesiastical time and place drop away as useless shell or indifferent garment. This is the reason why the works of great mystics have always been the world's favourite books of devotion."

The mystics of the Rhine valley, "Brethren of

* Hibbert Lectures.

the Free Spirit," " Friends of God," and other the like
more or less secret fellowships, produced an imposing
effect. Large congregations came together to their
preaching. Its results were shown, not in a great
organized movement, but in individual lives, in the
growth of independent thought. A movement like
that which piled on high the great Gothic cathedrals
was as much social and political as it was religious.
No such monumental result could arise from the
humbler labours of the mystics. Their teaching
tended in a different direction. Pomp of ceremonial,
and all of doctrine and circumstance that it involved,
was discordant with their feelings. Increased fervour
of private devotion, the ecstasy of the individual soul
in the privacy of a chamber, was their aim. Any
help towards this they fostered ; whatever had no
such tendency received no encouragement from them.

The city of Köln was the centre of life of the
mystic fellowship, especially during the last part of
the fourteenth and the first part of the fifteenth
centuries. Here then are some noteworthy dates.
Köln Cathedral was founded about the beginning of
the last quarter of the thirteenth century, and its
enormous choir was finished about the end of the
first quarter of the fourteenth century. Then the
building activity slackened. Years went by, and
little was added to the pile. The architectural spirit,
with all that it implied, ceased in the town about

the time of the consecration of the choir. Turn to
the last half of the fourteenth century, and what
do we see? No longer a building activity, but an
activity in painting. Meister Wilhelm and his
fellows are hard at work filling all the Rhine-land
with their pictures. That is the measure of the great
social, religious, and intellectual change, one of the
features of which was the prevalence and power of
mysticism.

In the Gothic age, as Wolfram's *Parcival* tells us,
the two chief centres of Northern painting were
Maastricht and Köln. Out of the Gothic school, from
these two centres, as power passed away from architecture to painting, there developed northwards the
Flemish school of the fifteenth century, and south-
wards the important schools of the Rhine valley, and
later of Franconia and Swabia. Now if the school
of Maastricht had left any considerable quantity of
remains, it would not be necessary in this place to
discuss the fortunes of the school of Köln; as it is,
however, we can do little more now-a-days than
reason from the one to the other. All the Gothic
schools, though presenting clearly-marked local dis-
tinctions, grew out of a single ideal. The more
northerly school was more individual, laid more stress
upon character and expression than her sister on
the Rhine, but in all main features the two were
much alike and followed similar lines of development.

'Moreover, as we shall see, in the fourteenth century most of the artists of the Low Countries were Germans from the Rhine valley, so that it is advisable to preface a study of the fifteenth-century Flemish artists with at any rate some short general sketch of the earlier school of Köln. Indeed, if we could begin by forming some idea of the art of the Rhenish district in the twelfth and thirteenth centuries, our conceptions of what is to follow would be all the clearer. But to do so we should have to inspect a number of far-scattered objects, accessible only with difficulty to the patient traveller. The fine enamels for the production of which Köln craftsmen were famous all the world over would have to be examined; the pages of many illuminated MSS. would have to be turned over, and the fading remnants of wall and roof paintings, such as those which decorate the churches of Schwarzrheindorf and Brauweiler,* would have to be hunted out. These works would have to be compared with the sculptured adornments of the Romanesque and Gothic buildings erected in the same period; and thus, eventually, sight and sense would be gained of the simplicity of style, the majesty of conception, and the confidence of faith with which Gothic artists went about their work. As the first years of the fourteenth century were approached, the progress of a change would be observed. Choosing,

* Copies in the Köln Museum.

for example, of the newer work, the painted decora-
tions of the now ruined church of Ramersdorf * in the
Siebengebirge, a new tendency would be apparent.
Graceful flow of line has become the painter's aim

THE WOMEN AT THE SEPULCHRE.   *Wiesenkirche at Soest.*
Thirteenth century.

in place of the old simplicity.   Moreover, the human
type changes.   The figures become more slender than

* They date from the end of the thirteenth century. There
are copies of them in the Berlin Print Room.

of old; the shoulders are made narrow, and the
bodies receive a peculiar bend. More important than
all this, a new fervour enters into the devotional
figures. There is no longer the same lack of self-
consciousness in the presence of the Deity, no longer
that perfect confidence in the Church's compact
between man and God. The individual now feels
that religion is an individual affair, and not a mere
matter of social organization. The next example of
the artistic productions of the day with which it
would be well to come in immediate contact, are the
wall-paintings on the screen round the choir of Köln
Cathedral. These were executed about 1322, that
is to say, just at the time when the building activity
flagged and the painting activity gained strength in
the Rhenish city. Architecture is still supreme in
these pictures. Figures and incidents are represented
l'ke coloured sculptures under sculptured canopies.
But the architecture is complex and pictorial in
quality, whilst the figures are less monumental, and
show more of the litheness and grace of life. There
are inscriptions below them, and amongst the letters
are little grotesque figures; but there is a difference
between the new and the old in this matter also.
The grotesque of the central Gothic epoch has a
largeness of vitality, an all-round reflection of life,
necessarily including some coarse elements. The
new grotesque is less all-sided, but in its restricted

sphere it is nevertheless perfect, very different from the gross and degraded conceptions of some of the fourteenth-century sculptors and miniaturists in England, France, and elsewhere. This Köln grotesque is full of play and grace, pure of heart and felicitous in fancy—a short-lived flower of art, tender and coy like some half-hidden violet of the dell.

Standing in the choir of Köln, the student should then raise his eyes to the clustered shafts which support its lofty vault. Backed against them and standing on brackets are a set of large statues of apostles, sculptured between 1349 and 1361. Having watched painting in the act of liberating itself from the control of sculpture, it would now be interesting to observe how sculpture is beginning to fall under the power of painting. Not only were these figures entirely painted over,—that had been the custom all through the Gothic age,—but they were *elaborately* painted. Their garments were covered with patterns of much complexity and rich colour. More important than this, the figures themselves have not the repose of their forefathers ; they are all bent this way and that. The attempt has been made to give them animation. Their drapery too is broken up into larger and more complex folds. All these things show the direction in which art was developing. The great age of architecture was passing away—the great age of painting was at hand.

D

With the year 1350 we approach the period of Meister Wilhelm and his followers. Meister Wilhelm, we call him, on the authority of a sentence in the old Limburg Chronicle, which mentions his name in connection with the year 1380, saying that Wilhelm lived about this time, who "painted a man as though he were alive." This reference is remarkable. It is the only record of the existence of the greatest artist of a great school ; but it is a record. It is a sign that artists were going to emerge from the anonymous state and to appear and attain fame as individuals. The art of previous centuries had been a socialistic art, an art of guilds and associations of men. The new art was to become an expression of individual feeling and individual skill. The words of the Limburg Chronicle, of course, set archæologists to work, hunting amongst the archives of Köln, and the result of their search is to prove this much—that a certain Wilhelm, born at Herle near Köln, a painter, bought a house in Köln in 1357, that he seems to have attained a prominent position among the citizens, and that he died about 1378. This Wilhelm of Herle was probably the same as Meister Wilhelm. It is customary to assign to him the best works of the Köln school, which, from internal evidence, we judge to belong to the period of his activity ; but it must be remembered that we have no documentary or other proof that definitely connects

THE ANNUNCIATION. *St. Clara Altar.* ASCRIBED TO MEISTER WILHELM.

his name with any known existing picture, except perhaps a ruined wall-painting at Köln.

The most extensive of the works ascribed to Wilhelm is an altar in one of the apse chapels of Köln Cathedral. It is called the St. Clara altar, from the church for which it was originally painted. This is the earliest important painting upon panel which has come down to us from the school, and it is visibly the work of a master hand. It manifests the simplicity in drawing and composition, the rhythmic flow of line, the tenderness of expression, the feeling for beauty of countenance, which are characteristic of the school. The altar consists of several panels bearing representations of incidents in the life of Christ. Here and there a sweet playfulness of heart finds early expression in them; as, for instance, where the Virgin holds the Child in motherly fashion over His bath, whilst Joseph pours water gently over His tender skin. The story of the life of the infant Jesus is told throughout like some idyllic tale of childhood in a poem.

Several more pictures in the Köln Museum link themselves with the St. Clara altar; not indeed as the work of the same individual, but as the work of the same school and period, expressing, therefore, the same sweet and mystical ideal. On a higher level than the rest stands the beautiful 'Madonna with the Bean-flower,' perhaps the best of all the works of the

Köln School, and certainly one of the sweetest old pictures in the world. It is always ascribed to Meister Wilhelm, and though this attribution is uncertain like

THE MADONNA WITH THE BEAN-FLOWER.   ASCRIBED TO MEISTER
WILHELM.

the rest, yet it is more convenient to adhere to it than not to have any simple designation for the great artist who painted it.   It may be grouped with two other pictures, probably the work of the same hand,

and both representing St. Veronica with the sweat-cloth bearing the impress of the face of Christ, the one being at Munich, the other in the National Gallery. A 'Madonna with a Bean-flower' amongst the pictures at Nürnberg likewise belongs to this group.

The Köln Madonna may be aptly used to illustrate the ideal of the mystics and the effect it produced upon art. In thirteenth-century sculptures and paintings we generally find that the figures of Virgin and Child are treated with great dignity as becomes Divine beings. Already, however, before that century had worn to a close, sculptures were made, such as the *Vierge dorée* of Amiens, in which the human element is a definite factor, and the mother's delight in her babe finds clear expression. The Köln painters, however, went further. A first glance at the 'Madonna with the Bean-flower' shows the wide difference that separates it from the dignified Gothic works. It is addressed not to the thronging masses of the folk, but to the individual worshipper. The spectator will enjoy it best alone. Its place is not over the high altar of a church, but in some oratory of private devotion. It is a thing to be seen often and contemplated long. This Virgin is not an exalted queen, but an amiable and tender friend, who attracts love rather than homage, and will return the protection of love rather than the protection of power. Clearly into this presence the worshipper must bring utter purity of heart. Fervour of devotion will naturally be called forth by such an ideal as this—higher in some respects, more restricted in others, than that of the central Gothic epoch.

The religion of the thirteenth century was one for free use at every moment of every day. It mingled in and tended to sanctify every act of life. Barter and sale, manufacture and war, alike presented their religious aspect at that noble time. But if thereby the actions of life seemed to receive a Divine sanction, the ideals of faith tended also at times to be draggled in the mire. As soon, at any rate, as the enthusiasm of the Gothic faith lost some of its vitality, this dragging down of religion became evident to the more spiritually-minded, and a reaction arose against it which produced the driving forth of the mystery plays into the market-places, and other similar changes. The movement of the mystics was a part of this reaction. In one sense they sundered religion from out-of-doors life. They sundered it in fact though not in intention. They laid stress upon a change of heart rather than on religious acts. They put the great emphasis not on the outward functions of the Church, but on the inward emotions of the heart. The acts of life were indeed to manifest the changed heart, but the change took place in the heart alone, and was wrought in silence and privacy. Thus private contemplation and private devotion were

raised to the first place, whilst public worship sank
to a lower level. The necessary worldliness and
pomp of ceremonial of the older and larger symbolic
religion were naturally distasteful to these forerunners of the Reformation. Hence the peculiar
type of this mystical Madonna. She clearly could
not be the Madonna of a German market-place.
This ideal could not be dragged down into the
handlings of the shop. The man inspired by her
could scarcely rise to be a great manager or leader of
men. He might be a sweet poet, an enthusiastic
teacher, even a pensive student, but he could scarcely
be a man of action, or, if he were, his hours of action
and of worship would be sharply sundered in spirit.

It would be easy to add a catalogue of pictures
more or less similar to this one, but our object here
is merely to draw forth the ideal from its material
expression, and for that purpose one example is as
good as many. Moreover, a class of pictures peculiar
to the Köln school, called ' Paradise Pictures,' claims
its share of attention. In the dreams of the mystics
the gardens of paradise were the home of a saintly
company, amongst whom the Virgin dwelt as queen.
Dorothy and Cecilia, Catherine and Barbera, and
many another virgin saint, were thought of by these
gentle-hearted folk as the sweet handmaidens of the
Virgin, the fairest and the purest amongst the fair
and pure. Their home was no place of stately

solemnity and rigid rule, but a bright and happy
garden, where, there being no impurity, there was
nothing but joy and brightness and peace in the
everlasting day.   Flowers blossomed on every hand,
and they plucked them in basketsful for the beautiful
Infant of their love.   They could sit down and talk
together in the bright meadows, and never a cloud
darkened the sky, never a cold wind blew, never a
scorching ray annoyed, but always gentle light and
murmuring breezes made fair sights and sounds
wherever they went.   So in the Köln pictures of the
fourteenth century Mother and Child are always
happy together, and conscious of each other's joy.
The Babe in the 'Madonna with the Bean-flower'
strokes the Virgin's face and looks up at her.   The
Virgin is always filled with a peace that has known
no breaking; and her maidens are like her.   Their
hearts are perfect.   The spirit of their home is the
spirit of their lives.   Their actions are thus always
free and unconstrained, yet they are in perfect
harmony, each with the other, and all with the wishes
of their Queen.

There exist a considerable number of Paradise pictures ; it will suffice then if a few are chosen as representatives of the rest.   A little winged picture at Berlin *
is perhaps the earliest which has come down to us.
It is very like the works ascribed to Meister Wilhelm,

* Phot. Berlin Photographic Co.

and certainly belongs to his school and period. Here the Virgin and four female saints are seated upon a flowery meadow, the naked Child upon the Mother's lap playing with the flowers which Dorothy offers Him out of her dainty flower-basket. Catherine holds out a purse towards Him, as though she wanted a flower put into it. Barbera and Margaret sit by contentedly looking on. It is instructive to compare this picture with one of the Gothic altars of a century before, speci-mens* of which may be seen in the Köln Museum. In the earlier work the dignity of the Gothic faith and the consequent restraint of the architectural feeling which it nurtured reign supreme. Each figure stands under its own niche and holds its own emblem. The emblems mark the individuals in place of a name, and each individual represents some definite aspect of the perfect life. How different is the Köln artist's treatment of his theme! Take, for instance, the figure of Dorothy, and test it by her legend.†

Dorothy was a noble maiden of Cappadocia, fair and pious. When condemned to death for her faith she said, " Be it so ; the sooner shall I stand in the presence of Him whom I most desire to behold, the Son of God, Christ mine espoused ! His dwelling is Paradise ; by His side are joys eternal, and in His

---

* Phot. Crefeld (formerly Raps) of Köln.
† Compressed from Mrs. Jameson's *Sacred and Legendary Art.*

garden grow celestial fruits and roses that never fade."
On her way to martyrdom a youth, named Theophilus,
called to her mockingly, " Ha ! fair maiden, goest
thou to join thy bridegroom ?   Send me, I pray thee,
of the fruits and flowers of that same garden of which
thou hast spoken : I would fain taste of them !" And
Dorothy, looking on him, inclined her head with a
gentle smile, and said, " Thy request, O Theophilus, is
granted." Whereat he laughed aloud. When she
came to the place of execution she knelt down and
prayed ; and suddenly appeared at her side a beautiful boy, with hair bright as sunbeams.   In his hand
he held a basket containing three apples and three
fresh-gathered and fragrant roses.   She said to him,
" Carry these to Theophilus ; say that Dorothea hath
sent them, and that I go before him to the garden
whence they came, and await him there." And the
angel went to seek Theophilus, and found him still in
merry mood about Dorothy's promise. . And he set
before him the basket of celestial fruit and flowers,
saying, " Dorothea sends thee these," and so vanished.
And thereupon Theophilus was struck with wonder
and became converted, and presently sealed his faith
with his blood.

Gothic painters were satisfied when they had represented a fair maiden with a flower-basket in her hand
as symbol of the legend.   But the artist of the mystic
school felt freer to treat things in the light of his

THE VIRGIN IN A GARDEN.   *Frankfurt d M.*

fancy. He took the old symbols and made playthings of them. Dorothy, in the garden of Paradise, does not merely hold her basket as a symbol ; it becomes the toy of the celestial Babe. The old dignity is thus indeed destroyed, but a new and charming freedom takes its place. The new art is indeed smaller and more individual. It does not address a thronged city of worshippers, symbolizing (where it cannot express) the full-toned chord of their united worship in word and work. It is an art intended for the chamber, an art that becomes eloquent only to the prepared mind, an art of the hour and place of private devotion, when the devout soul has shut out the world and brought itself face to face with its invisible ideal. It is, in fact, the art of a religion of fancy rather than of a religion fit for the use of common men in a world of work.

The feeling which the Berlin picture so plainly shows could not fail to attain a more developed expression. Frankfurt possesses a little panel which gives evidence of this development. Instead of a flowery meadow it shows a garden walled about, the golden background being thus reduced to a small area. There are fruit trees and beds of flowers in the garden and a fountain of running water. Tame birds perch upon walls and twigs in fearless happiness. It is Dorothy's garden again, for Dorothy was an especial favourite with the mystic artists,—Dorothy and Cecilia and Elizabeth of Hungary for different reasons.

The Virgin sits on a bank of flowers, reading with
devout delight in some holy book. There is a table
by her side, with a napkin and fruit upon it. Her
little Boy sits before her on the grass playing on
Cicely's cithern. Dorothy gathers cherries from a
tree, and another saint drinks from the fountain.
Gabriel and two young knightly saints, George and
Maurice perhaps, are in one corner of the place, and
they have a monkey with them for their amusement,
after the fashion of young gentlemen ·of the day.
Everything is refined and courtly, for this is the
garden of the Court of Heaven, whither the Queen
goes forth after the banquet to divert herself with her
maids and pages of honour.

More famous than this picture is the Madonna in
Köln Museum ascribed to Meister Stephan ; but
there a new humanizing element is seen, working in
through the medium of Flemish influence. Another
no less beautiful Paradise picture is at Darmstadt
in the palace of Prince Karl. The perfect freedom
of the idyllic atmosphere did not last very long.
The figures gradually became more individual and
characteristic, at the same time drawing back into
something of the old reserve. Thus in a Madonna
at Berlin,* painted under the influence of Meister
Stephan, the relations between the different saints
are not so close and unrestrained as before. There

* Phot. Berlin Photographic Company.

is formality in the surroundings, and the figures lack
unity of occupation. Barbara alone has anything

THE MADONNA. *Köln Museum.* ASCRIBED TO MEISTER STEPHAN.

to do with the Virgin and Child, and her action
is confined to the formal offering of a pink, the

E

symbol of friendship. Into this picture a family of donors is introduced—a beautiful series of portraits —but they have the effect of removing the subject from the land of poetry and dreams and bringing it down to earth. The picture is very lovely both in idea and execution; it is better drawn than the earlier works, though perhaps not so well coloured, and it is painted on a larger scale; but though beautiful, and perhaps in its own way quite as beautiful as the Paradise pictures, it enshrines a new ideal, and proves that the power of mysticism was fading out of art within fifty years of Wilhelm's death.

Still the Köln painters retained for some decades much of the sweetness which the Mystics' ideal had taught them. They were the first, and for a long time they were the only, school of artists, who, under the name of incidents in the life of Christ, painted those charming pictures of sweet family life which still delight every spectator. About the year 1480 there was a painter working at or near Köln, who, his own name having gone into forgetfulness, has been cursed with the clumsy denomination, " Master of the Lyversberg Passion," because he painted the famous altar-piece once in the Lyversberg Collection and now in the Museum at Köln. A little panel by him at Nürnberg represents the Birth of the Virgin in so sweet and tender a fashion that it can hardly have ever been surpassed. The figures are very human ; the costumes and surroundings are those of the upper classes at the time ; but the tenderness of sentiment—where the new-born babe turns round to bless its mother—rises above the level of every-day life into the region of poetic thought, and this quality was an inheritance which the painter received from those forerunners of his who yielded themselves willingly to the influence of the " Brethren of the Free Spirit " and the " Friends of God."

Mysticism maintained itself longer in the Low Countries, the birth-place of its noblest product, the *Imitatio Christi;* but there, as we shall see, it did not affect the development of art. That development was directed by the stout merchants and craftsmen of the most practical country in the then world. Nevertheless, quite at the end of the fifteenth century, the old Paradise picture reappeared there once more, and had a short-lived currency. A Madonna * by Gerard David, now at Munich, is the best example of this singular revival. The landscape all about it is modern, and the costumes are modern, but the spirit of the thing is the spirit of Meister Wilhelm and his gentle followers.

The Paradise pictures have taken us away from the direct line of development, to which swift return must now be made. Meister Wilhelm died, and

* Phot. Hanfstängl.

anonymous painters arose in his place and carried his art to further technical completeness. The finest production of this second generation of artists is the famous Madonna in the Archiepiscopal Museum at Köln.* There the Virgin, larger than human, stands upon flowery turf, with the diminutive Elizabeth of Reichenstein, donoress of the picture, kneeling at her feet. Angels look happily over and support a curtain behind, while the Most High, the Dove, and a group of singing angels appear in the blue sky. The Virgin is sweet as she of the bean-flower, but with a more human sweetness; the Child is no other than a human babe, dressed in a little embroidered garment such as mothers love. There is a larger sweep in the drapery than of yore, and its form is modern. Then again the sky is not gold, but blue. The gold of the old backgrounds has taken refuge in the pattern of the damask hanging. The picture was painted about the year 1425 (to judge by the donor's apparent age), some half-century, that is to say, after Wilhelm's death. Changes had been taking place in the ideal of the Köln artists, though not very rapidly. The architectural element is gone from the design, the symbolical element is fast going. The donor of the picture is represented by her own portrait, not by the figure of her patron saint. On the other hand, most of the essential

* Well reproduced by the Arundel Society.

qualities of sweetness remain ; some are even increased in force. The Child is the infant of the
Paradise pictures, more lovely here than ever ; the
angels are his frolicsome little playfellows—incar-
nations of brightness and grace. The painter of
the picture is by some considered to be Meister
Stephan, with whom we shall hereafter have to deal.
To me it seems the work of a mature artist of the
generation intervening between Meister Wilhelm
and him.

Few, if any, schools of art have produced, even at
their height of power, a series of works in none of
which is there a jarring touch. Usually, even in the
works of great artists, we find some detail somewhere
which is out of keeping with the rest. But even
the second-rate artists of the Köln school in the
fourteenth century are wholly true. They paint like
men whose minds dwell uninterruptedly in one
atmosphere of perfect repose. They know nothing
about competition, they are not anxious for personal
renown, they never sign their names or declare their
presence, they are not in a hurry, they have no
eagerness after originality, they are careless about
novelties, they ask for no earthly immortality, they
are content with their station in life and the world
in which they live, they are satisfied with the simple
food and clothing they receive, and as for fame they
look for a higher reward than that, when one day

they shall enter into the very land they loved to picture, and the words of their greeting will be, " Well done, good and faithful servant, enter thou into the joy of thy Lord."

To modern eyes there may be something bounded and even mean in such work as this of the gentle artists of Köln. In our day every one wants to be rich, to possess as fine things, to dwell in as fine a house, to live in as splendid a style, as his neighbour. Hence results horrible misery of competition which has invaded society in what are called civilized countries, destroying all power of restful thought, and rendering odious to many that ancient ideal of a "peace that passeth understanding," which was nothing more than a foresight of the perfection of what already in their hearts men partially experienced. We have already travelled a long distance since the days of Meister Wilhelm. We have learnt many things and made many inventions which would have frightened his simple heart. But perhaps here and there in the backwaters of life there may be found even to-day one and another pure and peace-loving soul, to whom it will seem not impossible that all the science, the philosophy, the history, the inventions and discoveries made from that day to this, a mere drop as they are, not worth counting in the infinite ocean of the unknown, have been hardly purchased · by the loss of that holy and restful ideal which enabled Meister Wilhelm, and doubtless many more in his day, to live in unruffled peace of mind, satisfied with this world, and joyous in anticipation of a better which was certain to come.

CHAPTER II.

LONG before the fifteenth century, the blossoming period of Flemish art, the provinces of Flanders and Brabant were famous for their wealth throughout all Europe. Already in the thirteenth century a queen of France could say with disgust that the wives of the burghers of Ghent were as rich and as splendidly bejewelled as herself. This wealth the people of the Low Countries owed partly to the geographical situation of their land, but chiefly to their own national character. Part of their country was a redeemed swamp, which none but a hardy race could have chosen for a home. The energy which enabled them to beat back the ever-threatening sea was not likely to be satisfied with that conquest alone. An amphibious race, their ships soon found a way to an ever-widening circle of distant ports. Commerce came naturally to them, for their country was situated at one end of the trans-European trade-route which

led from Bruges to Venice, and thus linked England
and the Baltic ports with the cities of the Levant and
the distant East. But the burghers of Flanders were
not only carriers, they were makers too. They were
the weavers of Europe. Their ships brought them
raw wool, shorn from the backs of the sheep of the
Surrey downs, and these fleeces they wove into gold.
The Woolsack, upon which the Lord Chancellor still
sits, was symbolic of the wealth of England ; the
Golden Fleece, which Duke Philip the Good chose
as emblem of the order of chivalry founded by him
at Bruges, was symbolic of the industry of the Low
Countries. The history of the period with which we
are concerned is really the history of the Woolsack
and its Golden Fleeces.

The Bruges of to-day presents few signs of its
ancient splendour. Its public buildings have been
either battered or entirely removed, and of the
palaces of its merchant princes, the finest examples
of domestic architecture out of Italy, all have disappeared except two. In the fifteenth century buyers
and sellers from every land resorted to Bruges for
their trade. The merchant of Venice and the Jew
of Lombard Street encountered one another on her
quays and in her exchanges. Sailors and traders‘
from all parts of the world made her streets lively
with the varied colouring of their bright costumes.
They came and went, and each left something behind

him. The wealth of England met the wealth of the East in the market-halls of Bruges. The representatives of twenty foreign princes dwelt within the walls of this capital of the Dukes of Burgundy, at the cross-roads of the highways of the earth. In those days, says Mr. Weale, "the squares" of Bruges "were adorned with fountains; its bridges with statues in bronze; the public buildings and many of the private houses with statuary and carved work, the beauty of which was heightened and brought out by gilding and polychrome; the windows were rich with storied glass, and the walls of the interiors adorned with paintings in distemper, or hung with gorgeous tapestry. If but little of all this now remains, it must be borne in mind that, during the past three centuries, Bruges has seen its works of art exported by Spaniards, destroyed (when not sold) by Calvinist iconoclasts and French revolutionists, and carried off by picture-dealers of all nations."

Ghent, Louvain, Mechlin, Ypres, and several other neighbouring towns, were vast manufacturing centres. Louvain could muster 150,000 men, amongst whom no fewer than 4000 were master weavers employing from thirty to forty hands. The suburbs of the town were crowded. At Ghent the weavers' guild alone numbered 40,000 members. The city could turn out an equipment of 80,000 men. Day by day the great bell summoned the workmen to their tasks, and the

MAISON DES BATELIERS AT GHENT.

surging crowd that hurried forth rendered the streets impassable. Life in such towns flowed in no gentle current. It was impassioned. Civic feeling was intense. The token of a town's freedom and individuality was the belfry tower. Many of these towers remain, looking down in their hoary age upon the withered glory whose blossoming they beheld. Like some human being in a second childhood, they prattle aimlessly of the past, and at the old stated intervals some of them still chime forth the notes which once summoned the throng of thousands to their daily toil, or dismissed them at evening to their rest. Now no multitude listens to their call, but the hoarding of the bill-poster echoes it back in irreverent scorn.

The close knitting together of religious, social, and political life, which characterized the middle-ages throughout Europe, is very plainly exemplified by the organization of industry in the Flemish commercial centres. Going back beyond the limit of precise knowledge about social history, it is clear that, in very early days, when industries began once more to raise their heads after the anarchic period of the barbarian invasions, the workers in some places joined themselves together, by a loose kind of bond, for religious and social purposes. In time all the men engaged in a trade, or in two or three connected trades, were thus linked together into confraternities, the intention of which was often purely religious, the

members being bound to be present at the funeral
of any one of them, to pray for his soul, to attend
certain anniversaries, and so forth. These religious
services were no doubt often followed by social
gatherings; at any rate the bond once formed was
not slow to develop. It was the time when every one
had to struggle for his rights; when citizens were
wresting charters of self-government from their feudal
lords, and when every industry had to resist pillage
from all quarters. In this lengthy struggle men
with common interests had to stand shoulder to
shoulder for their common weal. Thus all the
workers at one trade fought together to obtain
favourable conditions for their work; and so, by
action, the society or guild, as it was called, became
strong. The guilds of a town presently included
most of the intelligent citizens. Community of
interest forced them to unite together against the
feudal lord. From this union of the guilds sprang
municipal government, the guild becoming the political unit. Thus guilds represented the three sides
of mediæval life, and were at once social, political,
and religious institutions.

For a self-governing municipality certain buildings
were necessary. A belfry was the first requirement,
and in early days its various storeys served for prison,
magisterial court, and record office. But as the
requirements of a growing town increased, a town-

hall had to be added to the tower. The oldest existing belfry is that at Tournay, whilst the finest is the famous tower of Ghent over which swings the Golden Dragon famed in story. The first of the fine town-halls was that at Bruges; it served as model for the still more elaborate edifice at Brussels, from which again the town-halls at Louvain and Audenarde were freely imitated. In addition to a belfry and a town-hall for governmental purposes, and of churches for religious purposes, two kinds of public buildings were still required,—namely, market-halls for the sale of various commodities, especially cloth, and guild-halls for the several trade guilds. Of cloth-halls the finest existing is the noble structure at Ypres, which was erected in the best age of architecture, and is one of the most splendid municipal buildings in the world. It is no longer required for its ancient purpose, and to-day serves as Hôtel-de-ville. The Market-hall connected with the belfry at Bruges is likewise a famous building, striking now-a-days as a monument of the city's former importance.*

The guild-halls unfortunately exist in very small numbers now. Traces of some of them can be found buried in the midst of modern plaster; as, for example, the Maison des Charpentiers at Antwerp. In Ghent two very fine guild-halls are fortunately

* See articles on Belgian Civic Architecture in the *Portfolio*, Nov. and Dec. 1884.

preserved, but even they are only battered specimens, and presumably could not compare with the splendidly-built and sumptuously-furnished houses which were the pride of the more wealthy corporations. Amongst the five hundred palaces of marble or hammered stone, burnt at Antwerp in the days of the Spanish Fury, many no doubt were guild-halls. But our interest now is not so much with the buildings themselves as the institutions they were raised to house. Guilds in the fifteenth century, whatever their first origin may have been, consisted of two classes, according as they were chartered or unchartered. The unchartered guilds were voluntary associations of men and women under the patronage of some saint, usually for a religious purpose. Such, for example, was the Confraternity of Our Lady of the Seven Sorrows founded at Bruges, the members of which possessed a chapel in the cathedral, paid a certain contribution in support of religious services held within it, bound themselves to fulfil stated religious duties, and participated in the spiritual advantages which this piety merited. Such confraternities were often formed for charitable purposes, supporting perhaps a hospital, or relieving the sick and the destitute. Sometimes they were of the nature of benefit or burial societies. At all events they were very numerous and multiform. There were also shooting societies, or clubs of men-at-arms, the members of which met together pretty

frequently, and indulged in sport and social intercourse. The three great shooting-places at Antwerp
were important sights of the town, and when Dürer
was staying there he tells of his being taken to
see them. Equally numerous throughout the Low
Countries were the guilds of the Rhetoricians. They
were associations of artisans for purposes of amusement. The members composed lengthy poems which
they recited to their society, and every year meetings
were held in this or the other town to which delegates were sent from all the country round. Dramatic
and musical exhibitions were also an important part
of their business. These guilds of Rhetoric in fact
performed many of the functions of the modern
periodical press, they attained considerable political
influence, and the Government, being unable to suppress them, did what it could to secure their help
by flattery.

The chartered guilds were, however, the most
influential. No man could work for pay in a town
unless he were a citizen free of the town. Moreover,
he was not allowed to exercise a trade unless he
belonged to the guild of that trade. It was only as a
member of a chartered guild that a workman occupied
a recognized and stable position. In the socialist-
ically-constructed middle-ages independent units
were regarded with little favour. Every man had to
join a recognized association before he could secure

F

his rights, and every association not only conferred rights but exacted the fulfilment of duties. The guild entered into, and influenced, every relation of the workman's life, and it is impossible to discuss any subject connected with mediæval industry without considering the guilds. Painting, to the mediæval mind, was a craft like any other, and was therefore organized in the usual way. A painter did not look upon himself and was not regarded as a person superior to ordinary discipline. It is only in times of decay that artists give themselves airs, and require to be considered in a Bohemian category of their own. In the great ages of art painters lived like other craftsmen, and were paid for the work they did according to a fair scale of remuneration. They lived simply, working unobtrusively and hard, and their work was first of all good, and next beautiful. That at any rate was the intention which the painters' guilds had in view—to secure good and honest work on the one hand, and to secure just and prompt payment for it on the other. The guild, therefore, first of all intervened in the education of the youthful artist. The lad had to be bound apprentice for a series of years to a recognized master of the craft, who from that day forward stood to him very much in the relation of parent to child. The master was responsible for the apprentice's education, moral and technical. The boy lived under his roof, served him at table, and about the house, and had to fulfil his bidding in all respects. The master, on the other hand, was bound to give him instruction in all matters connected with his craft. The methods of painting in those days included a numerous series of processes. The artist had to know how to prepare his panel, and what should be the nature and quality of the wood. Next, he had to be able to prepare and lay on the coating of fine plaster or *gesso* which formed the ground upon which the colours were laid. The evenness of this coating and the firmness with which it adhered to the wood, were important for the durability of the picture. Further, he had to know how to make every implement and every colour he wanted, for there were no artist's material shops in those days. Neither the method of *tempera*, nor the improved method of the Van Eycks, in which varnish was used as a medium for laying on all the surface colours, was a simple process. Moreover, the preparation of oils and varnishes required no small dexterity. Further, when engraving upon wood and copper-plate was invented, artists were at first expected to be able to design for the wood-cutter, and perhaps themselves on occasion to engrave a woodblock, and this involved a further knowledge of tools and processes, including some dexterity with the printing press. Moreover, any artist might be called upon to make a drawing, and that was in a day when cheap lead pencils did not exist. He might have to work with the silver-point, and then his paper required special preparation, which he had to give it with his own hand; or he might work in chalk or charcoal, and the selection of materials had then to be done by himself; there was no dealer to do it for him, unless the guild stepped in, as we shall see it sometimes did. The difference between ancient and modern artists is thus very great. The modern student has only to go to a shop, buy what his master tells him, and then learn to use it. The student in old days had to know how to make whatever he required. Certain colours indeed, like ultramarine which came from Venice and brick-red made in Flanders, could be bought; but artists had to know exactly what they wanted, and to be able to discriminate accurately for themselves between good and bad materials. There was no go-between to undertake the task of selection for them.

With so much to learn, a lad had a good five years' work before him when he commenced his apprenticeship, though in some towns the period was only three years; it varied according to the locality. If the master was an artist of real power, and the apprentice a lad capable of reverence, it is hard to imagine any arrangement better suited for enabling the one to bring his influence more powerfully to bear upon the other, and thus to secure greater permanence, and a better chance of expression, even after his own death, for the ideas that perhaps his technical skill had not been sufficient to formulate in works of art ; and for enabling the other to enrich his youthful and enthusiastic mind with seeds of thought and high ambitions beyond the power of his years. To take one instance out of many ; how much did Giotto owe to Cimabue over and above the meagre technical methods he learnt from him ? How many of the high ideals and noble conceptions embodied in the pupil's work years after the master's death, nevertheless owed their origin to the large heart and penetrating intellect of that master ? In the diaries and autobiographical sketches which Dürer has left us, we gain clearer glimpses than almost anywhere else into the inner life of a northern artist. He does not say much about his pupil days, except that his father delighted in him because he was diligent in trying to learn, and that in the workshop of his master Wolgemut, he had much to suffer from his fellow-apprentices. No doubt in those rough days a sensitive lad would not find his 'prentice days very easy, especially if he were one among several high-spirited boys. In that fashion, however, he had to gather his learning together, and results prove it to have been no very bad fashion either.

Apprenticeship ended, the youth emerged not yet a full artist, but a journeyman. He could now work for pay under any master he chose, and in some towns there were guilds of journeymen, though of course such guilds were not among the chartered bodies, and must not be confused with the regularly-organized painters' guilds with which we are now dealing. During his years of journeymanship the young craftsman frequently, I believe generally, went away from home and wandered to various towns, working everywhere for hire, and at the same time gathering experience of men and an enlarged knowledge of the various methods of his craft as practised in different localities. For an artist these years of wandering were of great value. He came in contact with a wider range of subjects than his own town could have supplied to him ; he saw the master-pieces of many great painters ; his eye was cultivated, and his hand, already disciplined to perfect obedience, was able to give permanent form to whatever struck him as worthy of note. Dürer probably went to Venice in his years of wandering, and at all events he travelled up the valley of the Rhine. This journey produced a marked effect upon him. Everywhere he had nature before him, and he studied her face with all the enthusiasm of youth in novel surroundings. He was away from parents and home for four years, about the usual duration of the period of journeymanship. At the end of that time any youth of ordinary industry and ability was in a position to take his stand as a com-

petent workman, fully prepared and educated in all
the foundation principle of his craft, and with eye
and hand practised to fulfil the bidding of the mind.

After giving proof of his abilities to the satisfaction
of the appointed officers of the guild, the workman
was now, upon payment of certain fixed fees, raised
to the status of a master of the craft. He had to
take solemn oaths of honesty, and to promise that
his work should be done as in the sight of God.
Henceforward he was a man; his status was fixed.
He had a vote along with his fellows for the appointment of the officers of the guild, and he had his share
in the property of the guild. His duties and rights
were definite. At this time also it was customary
for him to take a wife. His years of roving were at
an end; he was now to become a citizen and a house-
holder. But he was no more free as a master than
he had been before as apprentice or journeyman.
The guild, through its appointed officers, still continued to watch over his work. He was not allowed
to use any except recognized materials and tools.
If bad materials were found by the guild inspectors
in his possession, they were destroyed and he was
fined. He had to work according to the best known
methods, and any instances of scamping brought to
the knowledge of the authorities were rigorously
punished. The guild again stood between him and
his customers. Every contract he entered into had

to be registered in the company's books. His finished work had to be valued by the appointed officers, and if the price had been settled in advance they were called upon to state whether the work came up to the standard contracted for. In case of a dispute between the artist and his employer the guild officers were called in to settle it, and to see that an honest bargain was honestly fulfilled. When an artist bought raw materials he had to bring them to be approved ; when he bought tools he had to bring them to be marked with the sign of the guild. I remember a regulation of a certain guild of leather-workers, which provided that if any member was fortunate enough to acquire a lot of leather of more than ordinary excellence, he was bound to hand over half of it to the guild at the price he paid for it, so that his fellows might share his good fortune. This was a perfectly fair arrangement, because the moiety of luck which a man lost on one occasion was returned to him in fractions from the luck of his companions. Very likely similar regulations were enforced by painters' guilds. The guild, at all events in many places, acted as wholesale buyer, and retailed to its members at wholesale prices the materials they required for their work. But guild members were not restricted to purchasing from the guild alone. It was only when a favourable chance of buying a large quantity of materials occurred that the guild stepped in, and the members could share in the good fortune if they pleased. The various painters' guilds of the Low Countries were federated together by a loose sort of bond. At stated intervals delegates from all the guilds in the country met in some town or other, and spent a few days in social intercourse, discussing matters of common interest, and no doubt at such meetings new methods and improvements discovered in one part of the country were made known to the representatives of men working in other districts. The remarkable uniformity in types and processes used all over the Low Countries, which would otherwise be difficult of explanation, was doubtless due to this periodical meeting.

As the workman advanced in fame and in the confidence of his companions he became liable to election as an officer of the guild, and if elected he was obliged to serve. His duty might then be to collect the contributions of the members, not only those levied by the guild for its own purposes, but the taxes levied by the town and the State, for all of which the guild was responsible. Or he might be appointed to value work done, or to inspect the tools and materials used by the members. Large sacrifices of time might be required for these services, and the only reward given for them was the dignity pertaining to the position and the influence it carried with it. A guild officer was a man of consideration in a town.

The relations which the different guilds bore, one to another, were defined by law. Certain superior guilds interfered directly in the government of the town, whilst others did not ; and this distinction gave rise at one time to serious local disorders. Another question not settled without much litigation related to the crafts allowed to be exercised by the members of a guild. It occasionally happened that two guilds claimed the exclusive right of a certain kind of work. As a rule, the work which belonged to the members of one guild was forbidden to members of all the others. For example, there were separate guilds at Bruges for painters and illuminators. Painters were not allowed to make miniatures, and miniaturists were forbidden to paint pictures. The Guild of St. Luke included painters, saddlers, glass-makers, and mirror-makers ; that of St. John illuminators, calligraphers, binders, and *imagiers*. This division seems unnatural, but if we follow the history of the thing back to early times it is readily explained. The illuminators' guild was of much later date than that of the painters. Even before the illuminators were enrolled into a guild at Bruges, it was decided by a law-suit that illuminators might only use water-colours, and that the making of pictures in oil-colours, or with gold and silver, was the exclusive right of members of the corporation of painters.

The only exception to this rule was in the case

of an artist in the direct employ of the Sovereign.
He was allowed to do any work that might be
demanded of him without being called upon to make
himself a member of the corresponding guild ; for,
it must be borne in mind, a competent workman
could by payment become a member of any guild.
It was not necessary that he should have received
his education by serving apprenticeship to a master
of that particular guild. Once educated and capable
of proving himself a good workman, the payment of
an entrance fee made him free to work.

Such, then, was the nature of a guild in relation
to the organization of industry ; it was equally important as an institution for social intercourse. Very
few guild-houses remain in which the interior has
not been entirely changed ; but one at Lübeck contains the large room on the ground-floor in its old
state. That room was the meeting-place of the
guild-members. It resembled a tavern-parlour, and
is divided into bays, each with a table and benches
in it, something like the room in the famous " Cock "
eating-house in Fleet Street. There at evenings the
members came together to drink and converse after
the labours of the day. Compare these conditions
with the barrenness of a modern working-man's life,
and it will be admitted that the mediæval arrangement was far superior. On great days more elaborate
gatherings took place. The members and their wives

dined together, and sometimes entertained illustrious guests. Read, for instance, Dürer's account of the entertainment given to him by the Painters' Guild at Antwerp :—

"On Sunday, which was St. Oswald's Day (5th August, 1520), the painters invited me to their guild-hall with my wife and maid-servant. They had a quantity of silver plate, and costly furniture, and most expensive food. All their wives were with them, and as I was led in to table, every one stood up in a row on either side, as if they had been bringing in some great lord. Amongst them were men of very high standing, all of whom behaved with great respect and kindness towards me, saying that in whatever they could be serviceable to me they would do everything for me that lay in their power. And while I sat there in such honour, the syndic of the magistrates of Antwerp came with two servants to me, and gave me four cans of wine in their name, and said to me that they wished thereby to do me honour, and assure me of their good-will. For that I returned them my humble thanks, and offered them my humble services. Next came Master Peter, the town carpenter, and gave me two cans of wine with the offer of his services. When we had been long merry together, up to a late hour of the night, they accompanied us home in honour with lanterns, and prayed me to rely confidently on their good-will, and to remember that in whatever I wanted to do they would all be helpful to me. So I thanked them and lay down to sleep."

Such social gatherings, in which the newly-instituted young master could meet men of high position in the town on a footing of equality, were of great value, bridging over, as they did, the gulfs that tend to arise between different grades of society. Notwithstanding the aristocratic organization of mediæval life, the strong line of division between rich and poor did not then exist. That has been one of the most conspicuous products of the insane cry for "Liberty, Equality, and Fraternity" under the echoes of which the revolutionists of Paris banished the reality of all three from the soil of Europe.

Guilds further took an important part in all public rejoicings and festivals. If a prince were to be received in state, the guilds organized the reception, each undertaking its part. On the great *fête* days, the guilds marched in procession through the town, many of them adorning their part of the show with wagons bearing *tableaux vivants*, usually representing either some event in sacred history or an assemblage of emblematic figures. Of such processions the most famous were the *Omegang* at Louvain, and that which paraded through the streets of Antwerp on Lady Day. Dürer has left a description of the latter, telling how "the whole town was gathered together,

craftsmen and others of every class, each dressed in
his best according to his position. Every rank and
guild had its sign by which it could be known.
Between the groups (forming the procession) great,
costly candles were borne, and old-fashioned long
French trumpets of silver. And between were also
many pipers and drummers such as they have in
Germany. The whole was carried on with much din
and blowing of trumpets. I saw pass through the
streets, in ranks widely separated one from another,
the Guilds of the Goldsmiths, the Painters, the
Masons, the Broderers, the Sculptors, the Joiners, the
Carpenters, the Seamen, the Fishermen, the Butchers,
the Leatherers, the Weavers, the Bakers, the Tailors,
the Cobblers, workmen of all kinds, and many craftsmen and tradesmen who serve the needs of life. There
were likewise the merchants and traders, and all their
hands. Then came the clubs of men-at-arms with
guns, bows, and crossbows ; also the travellers and
pedlars. Then came the town watchmen, and then a
great company of very stately people, nobly and
costly habited. Before them, I forgot to say, went
all the religious orders, and some who had made
foundations, all in their various habits, very piously.
There was also in this procession a great body of
widows who support themselves with the work of
their hands, and observe a special rule. All of them
were clothed from head to foot in white linen made

specially for them, very pitiful to look upon. Amongst them I saw persons of high estate. Last of all came the Canons of Our Lady's Church, with all the priests, scholars, and treasures. Twenty persons bore the image of the Virgin Mary with the Child Jesus, adorned in the most gorgeous fashion, to the honour of the Lord God. In this procession were brought along many heart-gladdening things splendidly arranged. For there were many wagons with plays upon ships and other stages, such as the company and order of the Prophets; and then, from the New Testament, the Annunciation, the three kings upon great camels and other strange beasts most cleverly done; also how Our Lady fled into Egypt—most pious to behold, and many more things which for shortness I omit to mention. Last of all came a great dragon, whom St. Margaret with her maidens led by a girdle; she was specially pretty. St. George came after her with his esquire—a fine knight in armour. Also there rode in this company youths and maidens beautifully and expensively dressed according to the fashion of many countries, representing various saints. From beginning to end this procession took more than two hours to pass by our house, and in it there were such a number of things that I never could write them all in a whole book, so I leave well alone."

Such being the chief industrial and social aspects

of a mediæval guild, let us consider for a few moments its religious functions. In the first place it must be borne in mind how great importance the manner of a man's death and burial and the prayers afterwards offered up on his behalf had in the opinion of the people of the fifteenth century. It was easy enough for a rich man to make arrangements for the foundation of memorial masses for the delivery of his soul out of the pains of purgatory, but less well-to-do folk had not the same facilities. Here, then, the guild stepped in, and its work in this respect was by no means the least important, in the opinion of the men of those days. The guild first of all either owned a chapel outright, or rented one from the authorities of some church. This chapel they furnished with an altar, an altar-piece, curtains for the same, chalice, patena, and so forth, for the service of the altar, vestments for an officiating priest, deacon, and sub-deacon, and often a good many more things besides. All these were the property of the guild, not of the church; and they are always mentioned in the inventory of a guild's substance. In addition to this chapel, the guild secured and paid for the services of officiating clergy on certain occasions, the payments being frequently made in accordance with a regularly drawn up and signed agreement, which stated with utmost minuteness what the services were to be, and with what elaboration of music, candles, and the like they were to be performed. On certain occasions commemorative services were held for the souls of all those members of the guild who had passed away. If a member of a guild died in poor circumstances he was duly buried with all Christian rites at the expense of the Fraternity. Connected with these directly religious acts the guild likewise exercised charity in its corporate capacity. If the widow and children of a member were left destitute, it was often the custom to relieve them at the expense of the whole body and to see to the education of the children.

The existence of this religious side in a guild produced an unforeseen but important result. If a rich man wished to found a memorial mass or other service in perpetuity he often preferred to leave his money in trust with some guild, which was bound to see that his intentions were carried out, and to be present in person at the said service. In return for this they likewise received a certain sum by the same agreement. A good deal of property came in this way into the hands of the guilds, and thus the governing body grew in importance. The ordinary revenues of the guild were derived from contributions levied upon the members and fees paid at entrance. The tendency of all such corporate bodies in those days was to grow rich. Their wealth, however, though partly spent in good cheer, was in the main devoted

G

to the furtherance of the interest of their special craft. The guilds of the City of London are almost the only ones that survive to the present day, maimed in every respect except their wealth and their feasts, but to the historian picturesque institutions of great value.

In conclusion, it may be well to note briefly some of the principal effects which the guild system produced upon the person of the artist, and thus upon his art, for all art is but the product and reflection of the conditions of the artist's mind, and the manner of its working. And first of all, in contrast to the present day, we may note the absence of the effects of competition. Works of art produced for exhibitions labour under the great disadvantage that they must be made striking. Amongst the multitude of their companions they must make their mark. This accounts for much of the flaring colour, the exaggerated drawing, the theatrical sentiment of current art. The old art of the guilds was quiet and reserved. The workman was taught to make his work first of all things good. To produce what was a piece of sound workmanship was of more importance than to paint a striking picture. The pictures required in those days were either altar-pieces or portraits. Both had needs be durable. The altar-piece was intended to last as long as the memorial mass founded by the pious donor—one and the other were to be permanent. Dürer says with just pride of one of his pictures, that 300 years hence it would be as fresh as the day he painted it; and so in truth it would have been had not the flames devoured it. More important still was the fact that the absence of the stimulus of direct competition left the mind of the artist freer. He had not to compete in expenditure with his fellows, as almost everybody does in the present day, either consciously or unconsciously. The mere making and spending of a little more money would in no wise have bettered his social standing. His rising in the world was in the main dependent on the opinion his fellow-artists had of him, and that opinion depended upon the soundness and workman-like quality of the thing he made. All these conditions were favourable to the development of a school of art whereof thoroughness was a virtue. It was not merely the result of chance that the brothers Van Eyck invented their peculiar method of painting by which they were enabled to produce pictures of almost unlimited durability and of unsurpassable finish, provided sufficient care were bestowed upon the work. The spirit of the day and the method of the day were reflections one of another. When men live in a scramble, they will paint in haste and buy in haste. In old days they went more leisurely to work. Take any picture of this old Flemish school and regard it carefully, you will find that only so do its beauties strike you at all. At the

G 2

first glance you are liable to pass it by. When you get to know it a little you find it impresses you more strongly, till at last you cannot but pause long and often before it in wonder and admiration at the depth of the artist's thought, and the completeness with which it is expressed. This completeness is due to the essential character of the artist's environment; it will be found everywhere where similar conditions obtained. Many of Jan van Eyck's pictures must have taken him months to paint; some of them not less than years. Dürer, who came rather later than the period now under consideration, but whose spirit was singularly like that of the Flemish artists, spent the greater part of seven years over six pictures. A man was not continually wanting to go on to something fresh. Every work he planned he intended to be monumental, and so he did his planning with care as became a thing of dignity. The spirit in which the work was done and the method of doing it reacted one on another, It is related that once when Jan van Eyck had half-finished a picture, and was drying it in the sun, the heat cracked it in half. This misfortune is said to have led him on to the invention of his improved method of painting. Something of the kind may well have been the case. Careful work implied that the results obtained should be certain and durable. A man would never be likely to hurry over the preliminary stages of that which was going to be his chief business for months. The silver-point drawings of the school which have come down to us, most of them probably the work of pupils drawing from finished pictures rather than, as gallery directors would often have us believe, artists' original studies— these very pupil drawings manifest the same careful spirit, and show how from the very first it was instilled into the youthful mind.

The other arts of the day give proof of the existence of a similar spirit in the workers devoted to them. Little remains of the splendid old Flemish jewellery, perhaps the finest goldsmith's work of which we have any record ; but what there is shows an elaboration and minuteness of finish that will be sought for in vain elsewhere. Never do we find any purely mechanical detail of ornament ; never, as in the jewellery of to-day, any mathematical arrangement of stones or ponderously brutal setting of massive metal. The charm of all this ancient work is in the living spirit that inspires it. The golden wreath, never directly imitated from nature, shows in its forms the same principle of growth that gives grace to a tendril and beauty to a leaf. Stones are set together not because they exactly balance one another, but because their colours form a perfect harmony. According to modern ideas the value of a string of pearls is in direct proportion to the closeness of similarity between the beads. According to ancient notions dissimilarity of colour and form would have been more admirable—not, however, dissimilarity of a mere chance character, but such a dissimilarity between adjacent members as gave to the whole sequence a rhythmic flow. The charm of old jewellery lay, however, not so much in the stones as in the artistic work of the setting. The precious metals were regarded as precious, not because of their rarity, but for the beautiful plastic qualities they possessed. Gold was treated as a fine clay which could be coaxed into the daintiest forms. The old goldsmiths were in fact sculptors working on a small scale, but producing forms as lovely as any that graced a mediæval building.

Consider, then, the tapestry weavers. Flemish tapestry is distinguished from all other kinds by the fineness of its thread. It is free from the roughness of texture usually so unpleasant in storied hangings. The threads are all fine and the web close. Such work, of course, took a great deal of time, but then time is of secondary importance to men for whom good work is the great consideration. Old Flemish tapestries have of course faded to some extent, but in other respects they retain their beauty to the present day, and are unsurpassed. Without directly resembling or imitating pictures, which no good tapestry can do, they possess the pictorial qualities possible to that kind of work, carried to an extraordinary point of finish. This finish is attained by the employment of a large number of different shades of coloured threads, mixed together with elaborate diligence, by workmen labouring in a peaceful frame of mind.

The Flemish artisans of the fifteenth century lived in outward turbulence and yet in inward peace. Hot and headstrong in the assertion of their common rights and freedoms, they were individually phlegmatic. They wanted only to be let alone to do their work to the best of their power. Their life moved like a strong-flowing stream in majestic evenness along its appointed course. But if a barrier was interposed against it, straightway there arose a surging and a roaring and a great transformation. The latent power burst forth with a fury terrible to behold; fair banks and smiling meadows were devastated in sudden and unconquerable rage, until the obstruction was swept away and the ancient channel again restored Thus confidently in the cities of Flanders the life of the folk went forward towards its mysterious merging into the ocean of eternity. Blindly, if you will, these men of iron plied their daily tasks—blindly, and yet, so far as faith is concerned, not so blindly as we. Nay! had they possessed no other faith than the confidence in honesty, which held their horny hands in disciplined restraint, they would yet be enviable amongst the sons of men. But they were also full of that ancient virtue of reverence which we have been taught to regard as "the chief joy and pride of life," yet which so regarding we little practise. They did always the thing that was within their powers, striving indeed by daily industry to increase the strength of those powers, but never hoping either by luck or momentary insanity to attain anything unattainable by patient thought and long-continued labour. "Patient continuance in well-doing" was the open secret of their success, and the standing protest they have left behind them against the faults and follies of all "fickle and perverse generations."

CHAPTER III.

PHILOSOPHERS and Historians, for the last half-century or so, have preached us a lengthy sermon upon the one word—Progress. They have told us that the History of Mankind is the history of an evolution; that whilst succeeding generations have come and gone, the work of each has been the production of an offspring finer than itself. They have painted society as a great organism, increasing in complexity with the tale of its years, increasing also in knowledge and power. Whilst accepting the general lines of this theory as a working hypothesis, the historian of Art is mainly concerned to insist upon certain visible facts, which his scientific colleague is apt to overlook. The historian of Art has it continually forced upon him that, with the growth of civilization, the artistic power of the human species by no means continually increases. What was possible to a less developed generation is impossible to one more advanced ; and indeed it is hard to avoid the conclusion that the artistic powers of the human race, far from increasing in periods of general progress, may often notably diminish. It would seem, then, that certain forms of art-production, beautiful enough in themselves to excite the wonder and reverence of succeeding ages, are possible only to a semi-developed race, and demand an order of intellect inferior to that of the after-coming men, who yet must bow before them in delighted awe. Art, in fact, gains very little from the progress of science. The discoveries of the last century have added nothing to her power, have brought no new spheres within her domains. She discourses not of science but faith, not of the thing known but the thing hoped for, not of the world of fact but the heaven of fancy. She looks upon the earth and it blossoms into Paradise, upon the face of man and it is as the face of an angel. Hence the art of any generation depends not upon its knowledge, but upon its Ideals of Faith and Hope ; and it would seem that these ideals diminish in beauty as the universe of the known increases in extent. No day, therefore, can produce the Art of a preceding age, because no day can feel the ideals of a day that is dead. The hopes of a man change with every rising sun ; the day that passes is taken out of the golden age of hope and added to the less attractive kingdom of knowledge, and often of disappointment. The present delight may to-day be enshrined in picture or poem, but not to-morrow, for then it has become a memory, perhaps even a bitter one. And, as with the individual so with the race, the ideal passes and with it passes the art it called forth. Later ages may look back with a memory for the one and a delight for the other, but the thing that was then made can be made no more : the art has passed away, and another takes its place.

The history, therefore, which it is our business to study, is a history of the succession of arts, or, if you like, of the succession of Ideals. At one period sculpture is the shrine of noblest thought, at another painting, at another music, at another the drama or the novel. This history of the succession of the arts remains as yet not only unwritten but unsketched. Each art has a period of rise whilst its predecessor declines ; each has a period of culmination, when all the minor arts of the day range themselves in subordination about it ; each has a period of decay, when its strength is gradually transferred to the new art which is to come. Thus about the beginning of the twelfth century the art of Gothic architecture arose in Europe, bearing sculpture and painting in her ministering train. In the thirteenth century architecture culminated, and produced such wonders of perfection as the cathedrals of Paris, Amiens, and Rheims, wherein the whole edifice was voiceful with perfect harmony of sculptured tympanum, tinted wall, and storied jewellery of glass. In the fourteenth century the power of architecture began to be taken from her. Painting ceased to be her obedient handmaid, rebelled against the restraints she imposed, and finally in the fifteenth century became herself acknowledged mistress of all the living arts. Slowly the artists' ideal changed. Slowly they forsook the contemplation of eternal mysteries, and opened their eyes to look upon the world of nature and the visible mystery of man by which they were continually surrounded. The painting of portraits supplanted the painting of Madonnas, and then the change from Henry the Eighth's Holbein to the Elizabethan dramatists was one that might almost have been foreseen. The introduction of music into the play involved no wide step, and once introduced its development was assured. Once more the servant is seen supplanting the mistress; the sceptre fell from the hand of the drama and was taken up by music.

At the present time, and probably for many years to come, we shall do well to confine our attention to the consideration of particular schools and epochs of art, one by one; but the student must continually bear in mind that the knowledge thus acquired is only so many links in a long and unbroken chain, the whole of which we hope one day to disentangle, and then by means of it one more anchor will be

ST. ELIGIUS. BY PETRUS CRISTUS. *Köln.*

cast forth into the invisible depths of the past, grant-
ing a firmer hold upon that infinite mystery over
which we float on the rising tide of time.

In this chapter, then, the Flemish art of the fifteenth
century shall be considered from the point of view of
the ideal which gave birth to it. The principal artists
of this school, whose names are known to us, were
Hubert and Jan van Eyck, Roger van der Weyden,
Hugo van der Goes, Hans Memling, and Gerard David.
On a somewhat lower level come such men as Petrus
Cristus, Thierry Bouts, and perhaps Gerard van der
Meire. The principal works in England belonging
to this school are,—by Jan van Eyck, the portraits of
the Arnolfini, and two men's portraits in the National
Gallery, the Thomas à Becket at Chatsworth, the
Madonna at Ince Hall, another at Burleigh House,
and another belonging to Mr. Beresford-Hope, also
Lord Heytesbury's St. Francis receiving the *stigmata ;*
of Petrus Cristus, there is a portrait belonging to
the Earl of Verulam, and a portrait of Marco Bar-
barigo in the National Gallery; to Gerard van der
Meire, Crowe and Cavalcaselle ascribe with little
reason the Deposition of St. Hubert in the National
Gallery; of Van der Weyden there is a triptych at
Liverpool, and another at Grosvenor House; of
Memling, there is a Madonna at Chiswick, and two
more in the National Gallery, besides two portraits
belonging to Mr. Vernon Smith; lastly, by Gerard

David, is a panel with three Saints in the National Gallery, and a triptych by his wife belongs to Mr. Willett at Brighton.

From the Van Eycks to David, a period of about a century, a great change is of course observable, but one Ideal reigns throughout. The general tendency of the change is the expression of the gradual alteration (development if you like to call it so) of the Ideal. This Ideal is, of course, most clearly and nobly expressed in the master-works of the school, and it will be well to glance at some of them to discover it there. From the Van Eycks we choose the upper part of the Ghent altar-piece as probably the work of the elder brother, Hubert; and the Louvre picture of the 'Madonna with Chancellor Rollin,' * certainly the work of Jan. From Roger van der Weyden we take the Middelburg altar-piece at Berlin.† From Hugo der van Goes the altar-piece in the hospital of S. M. Nuova at Florence.‡ From Memling the diptych known as Martin Nieuwenhoven's at Bruges;§ and from Gerard David the beautiful panel in the National Gallery.‖ Now, whatever the subject of these pictures, it will be found that the parts which soonest attract and most forcibly hold the spectator's attention are the faces, and

* Phot. Braun.   † Phot. Berlin Phot. Co.
‡ Phot. Alinari, Florence.   § Phot. Nohring.
‖ Phot. Braun and Berlin, Phot. Co.

especially the faces of the men. The eye rapidly passes on from the Madonna and Child to the kneeling donor, or the adoring shepherds. It is attracted to them, not on account of any fervent expression of devotion they betray, nor because of their physical beauty. The attraction is the result of a wider and deeper power, possessed to a remarkable degree by all these artists—their power of insight into character. The pictures they paint delight us in proportion to the portrait-like nature of the figures they introduce. The more they give way to their natural instinct, the more play they allow to their inherited delight in man and the face of man for its own sake, the more general and strong is the admiration they receive. Few Flemish paintings of the fifteenth century are more popular than the 'Madonna with Chancellor Rollin,' and yet the Virgin possesses no physical attractions; the Child is ugly, and the Chancellor hideous. In Van der Weyden's 'Nativity,' beauty of form is little more prominent, and the kneeling Treasurer Bladelin certainly does not come of a handsome stock. The 'Nativity,' by Hugo van der Goes, contains many faults of composition and no beautiful figures; but the adoring shepherds, ugly in feature and awkward in gesture as they are, attract and delight the eyes of all. In Martin Nieuwenhoven's diptych, it is by no means the erect and impenetrable Virgin that charms, but rather the

H

figure of the praying youth. Finally, of the four heads in Gerard David's panel, the most interesting are the two which approach nearest to the reflection of some living model.

We may go a step further, and say that amongst portraits those of men are better than those of women, and amongst the portraits of men the handsome are less excellent than the plain. None of the artists, about whom we are speaking, cared to look for well-formed features or well-built figures. There is no evidence that beauty of form was for them even a subsidiary aim. The vigour of their minds was engaged in grappling with a harder problem—the comprehension of the character of man. Not so very long ago, portrait painting was considered a secondary branch of the painter's art. What were called historical subjects were alone thought to attain the highest rank. The teaching of the last quarter of a century has succeeded in reversing this narrow judgment. It is now admitted that the highest subject a painter can choose is the face of man. The manner in which such work is to be undertaken has been roughly blocked out by Carlyle in the following granitic sentences:—"It is not the untrue imaginary Picture of a man and his life that I want . . . but the actual natural Likeness, true as the face itself, nay *truer*, in a sense. Which the Artist, if there is one, might help to give, and the Botcher never can ! Alas,

FROM THE ALTAR OF THE CANON VAN DER PAELEN. BY JAN
VAN EYCK. *Academy at Bruges.*

and the Artist does not even try it; leaves it altogether to the Botcher, being busy otherwise! Men
surely will at length discover again, emerging from
these dismal bewilderments in which the modern
Ages reel and stagger this long while, that to them
also, as to the most ancient men, all Pictures that
cannot be credited are—Pictures of an idle nature;
to be mostly swept out of doors. Such veritably,
were it never so forgotten, is the law! Mistakes
enough, lies enough, will insinuate themselves into
our most earnest portrayings of the True: but that
we should, deliberately and of forethought, rake
together what we know to be not true, and introduce
that in the hope of doing good with it? I tell you,
such practice was unknown in the ancient earnest
times, and ought again to become unknown except
to the more foolish classes!" (Friedrich). Without
pausing to discuss the general tone of this passage,
it may be remarked in passing, that the Flemish
pictures of the Madonna and Saints were, to the men
of the fifteenth century, eminently "pictures that
could be credited." But let us consider for one
moment the remarkable phrase which states that the
Likeness should be "true as the face itself, nay *truer*
in a sense," for herein lies the difficulty of the portrait-
painter's task. It is matter of universal experience
that under the influence of strong emotion certain
qualities of a man's character stand plainly written

upon his countenance. Other qualities require for their clear outward manifestation a gentler provocation. Seldom indeed does the face of a man tell his whole character at a glance even to the keenest observer. It is for this reason that photography can rarely succeed in producing a portrait, for any likeness worthy of the name must seize the face and posture of the person portrayed at the moment when the features are alive with thought and the limbs held in tension by the mind. A portrait painter has to watch his subject through many hours and under varied circumstances; he has to learn the orbit of every gesture, and to treasure up in his memory even the twinkle of an eye. He must carry on his observations till the whole man in his entirety becomes clear in his artist's eye, till he sees through the veil of outward form into the inner sanctuary of thought, till each gesture becomes an understood portion of an articulate language, each passing expression of the countenance the shadow of a comprehended thought. He has only now to set down the image which is clear in his own mind. He has to depict his subject, not necessarily as he beheld him at any moment, but as he might be at his best; the eye bright with the sympathy the artist has seen it express; the mouth trembling to utter a weighty word; head, hands, and limbs in those postures which are natural to them when the man is at his best.

Truth must be the sole aim of the portrait-painter, and yet truth of so high and magnanimous an order that it rises far above the petty imitation of a wrinkle or a scar, and pauses not until it surveys in wide-reaching view the whole area of the character of the man. The Ideal in portrait-painting, as in all other art, is only the highest comprehension of the real and true. Strive not to make a hero; strive rather to comprehend a man. Even that is a transcendent task. Paint the orator in the full-tide of his elo-quence; paint the poet as "enveloped in mist and with faltering voice" he goes his way, "rejoicing in life"; paint the merchant in the midst of honest busi-ness; the General in the hour of battle; the peasant in glorious command over his servant the soil. The orator cannot stand still for you, or the spell is broken; the very ploughman becomes another being when he ceases from his toil; to the sympathetic insight of a gifted seer is it alone possible to trace for lasting instruction the shadowy lineaments of passing thought.

When, therefore, we say that the painters of the fifteenth century in Flanders excelled in their por-traits, we give them the very highest praise, and thereby declare them worthy to be ranked among the great artists of the world. Portraits by masters of this school possess the quality of instantaneousness. They show their subjects caught in the middle of a

thought. They render, not only the dull scaffolding
of a countenance, but the fluttering drapery of expression it is wont at characteristic moments to put
on. Casting an eye over the pictures of this class
which have come down to us, we find that all the
faces portrayed possess many qualities in common.
They are all visibly men of one age and culture.
They are not fine of figure nor graceful of limb, but,
with hardly an exception, their faces tell us that they
are men of tried capacity and learnt experience.
Through the eyes of many of them glances a happy,
childlike soul enough, but the mind is almost in-
variably a slow-moving, solid power. They are men
of strength, capable of planning and carrying out
mercantile ventures, not unattended by risk, involv-
ing foresight, skilful handling, and honesty. Men
of the kind we can well conceive as having been fit to
lay the foundations of that commerce which we hold
in trust to-day. And such as they were the artists
who painted them ; they possessed the same industry,
they admired the same qualities. The virtue of
honest strength, which made the men of Flanders the
merchant princes of Europe, was the virtue whose
traces the artists of Flanders loved to observe, and
to set down with industrious veracity on their panels.
Their ideal is an ideal of strength. They love the
character whose essence is its force. They care little
for mystery, little for pity, little for enthusiasm, little

for any of the virtues which poets for the most part love to sing and painters to portray. They love a man whose visage tells of the strength of his character, who has weathered the buffetings of many a storm, and bears on his visage the marks of the struggle. They are true descendants of the worshippers of Woden and Thor—sons of the hammer rather than the bower, children of the war-cry, not minstrels of song. They love strength and eagerly seek for it. The myrtle-groves and laurel shades of the promised kingdoms of light they leave to the mystic dreamers of Italy. If angels dance it is in a heaven other than theirs; the best they ever hope for is a land of fertile meadows and well-built towns, where only light clouds deck clear blue skies, and where amongst the grass their own wild flowers flourish in profusion, overshadowed perhaps here and there by a tropical fruit-tree for novelty's sake.

They love strength, but, be it observed, strength of the mind, not of the body. They care little for a graceful Hercules, and even St. George is no special favourite with them. The man of their choice is indeed always large in bone and firmly knit together, certainly but not obtrusively strong. His chief feature, however, is the setting of his face. He may be stern and almost forbidding of aspect—they love him none the less; he is of the same brood as themselves. He may be stout; his wrinkles will

then become the more apparent. He may be grim
or good-humoured, sour or running over with laughter
—anything in short that is hearty and downright;
but a mystic dreamer like Francis of Assisi, a wild
enthusiast like Spanish Dominic,—these and the like
of these are altogether beyond the horizon of their
conceptions. A ragged John the Baptist they can
understand well enough; wandering about the wild
desert in his cloak of camel's-hair, half-starved, hollow
of cheek and lank of limb, his hair matted about his
head, his hands wrinkled, his eyes deep in their
sockets—him they are more or less in sympathy with;
but the mild John the Evangelist is out of their
sphere. They have to paint him often, but they
never paint him well; he is young and soft and
womanly, and they cannot treat him with success.
And so it is also with Christ the Man, the incarnation
of love, and pity, and enthusiasm of humanity.
Christ the Judge, Christ the King of Glory—Him
they can depict more grandly than ever it entered
into the heart of southern poet to sing, or artist to
frame. But Christ the tortured prisoner, the self-
sacrificing martyr, the tender shepherd of a wayward
flock—Him they successfully depict in no single
instance.

It is the strong and energetic character that they
love; and character grows in strength and definite-
ness with age, writing itself with daily increase of

visibility upon the face of a man as his years advance. The oft-repeated emotion moulds its memorial in plastic human clay. The brow held in constant tension by a thoughtful mind at length fails even in slumber to relax. Character writes itself by slow degrees on the wrinkles of the hand, on the pose of the members, nay, even on the creases of a shoe. Thus, for the student of character, the old face is more interesting than the open countenance of youth. For if indeed this is as yet unscarred by traces of failure and bitter disappointment, if it glows with hope and is bright with the consciousness of a boundless vista of unborn possibility, the other yet shows what has been done, however limited that may be. Its language is certain. For better or worse it is fact and experience that have written there their tale. The Flemish painter, therefore, treats with keener enjoyment and greater success the portraits of the old than of the young. If, as often happens, he is called to depict, on the wing of an altar-piece, the father and all his boys, it is upon the old man's face that all spectators will naturally be led to gaze. We all know many instances of a countenance, plain and unattractive in youth, but over which, in advancing years, a sweet indwelling character has spread visible, unavoidable charm. The subtlety of a settled expression, such as this, is far beyond the reach of many an artist, who yet can hold attentive before his pictures of girlish prettiness crowds of superficial admirers. Indeed, the student of character does not look to youth for the highest form of beauty, and the severest trial of a painter of character is the test of his treatment of middle age. An ordinary painter frequently makes his subject look younger than he is ; the character-painters of Flanders did exactly the contrary, and so also did one of the greatest character-painters of all, Albrecht Dürer of Nürnberg. In Dürer's portrait of Oswoli Krel * (at Munich) the face is so firmly held, in what must one day have become an habitual frown, that at the first glance it seems to be the face of a middle-aged man. A somewhat similar effect is produced in the finest of Roger van der Weyden's portraits, that of the young Count of Charolois, afterwards famous as Charles the Bold, who is introduced, as one of the three Kings, into the 'Adoration of the Magi,' now likewise at Munich.† His figure is indeed that of a young man, but the strong, almost fierce expression of the countenance would rather befit the tragic field of Nancy than the presence of the Infant Light of the World.‡

The masculine Ideal of the Flemish painters was thus one of strong character ; to what feminine Ideal, then, did it correspond ? We have plenty of materials for rendering an answer to this question, the ideal

* Phot. Hanfstaengl.   † Phot. Hanfstaengl.
‡ Prince Carl at Darmstadt has a good old copy of this figure.

woman being in the majority of cases the main apparent subject of a fifteenth century picture. Even the most enthusiastic admirer of Flemish works will scarcely bid us declare their Madonnas and saints to be of a high order of feminine beauty. Their figures are tall, slender, and erect; their features are sometimes of faultless form, and yet they fail to charm us after the manner of women. It may well be that they seemed lovely enough to the people for whom they were painted, so did the Madonnas of Italy to the Italians; but whereas these still delight us with their everlasting beauty, those of the North, if they affect us at all, do so by means of other qualities. It must be borne in mind that the people of the fifteenth century still lived in an age when the language of symbols was rich and widely understood. Every flower was an emblem, every colour had its own special meaning, every accessory told a special tale. The figures of the Virgin are likewise symbolic in every part. Her high forehead and wide arching brows tell of her intellectual power, her rich long hair figures forth the fulness of her life, her slim figure and tiny mouth symbolize her purity, her mild eyes with their drooping eyelids discover her devoutness, her head, if bent, speaks of humility, if erect tells of her sovereign estate. The supreme and evident virtue which reigns in all these Madonnas is an absolute purity of heart. And it is this virtue which, in the eyes of the fifteenth century Flemings, was supreme over all other feminine qualities. Women might be hard and stern, possessed of little charm of presence or grace of deportment, so only they were spotlessly pure. Painters of the period, almost without exception, seek to express the presence of this quality. For its sake they smooth away many a wrinkle, and likewise for it they suppress many a bright charm. They often destroy the individuality of their subject, but they never fail to present her as calm and pure. Purity in women, indeed, is the natural correlative to strength and character in man. The harder the strife in which men have to engage, and the greater the endurance and sternness demanded of them, so much the more do they insist that the genius of their home shall be unspotted by contact with whatever is gross, worldly, and impure. If therefore it is found that Flemish portraits of women are for the most part of little attraction, the observer should bear in mind the facts of the case, and, while censuring, if he must, what is lacking, remember that the fault in the picture arose from virtues in the society for which it was painted.

There are a few excellent Flemish portraits of middle-aged matrons, supreme amongst which is that of the wife of Jan van Eyck.* She is represented at

---

* In the foreground on the left of the 'Seven Sacraments,' at Antwerp, ascribed to Roger van der Weyden, there stands a female figure borrowed from this portrait.

the age of thirty-three, but she has the aspect of a
woman of forty or more. She is not in any sense
beautiful, and never has been, but there is a quiet
look of competence, serenity, and homely virtue
about her, which well supplies the lack of more
striking attractions. The picture originally belonged
to the Painters' Guild of Bruges, and hung as pendant
to the portrait of her husband, which unfortunately
disappeared long ago. The two works together would
have been of high interest as portraying one of the
toughest and most characteristic of the men of the
great days of Flanders, and the woman whom he
chose for his life's companion, and who so nearly
approached his ideal of what a perfect woman should
be that when he painted the Madonna he took the
face of his wife for a model.

Second only to the excellence of the portraits in
the majority of Flemish pictures, is the charm of the
little landscape backgrounds. The fifteenth century
painters of Ita.y, with the exception always of the
Umbrians, cared relatively little about landscape.
Why men of such opposite character as the Flemish
and the Umbrians should have felt the charm of
natural scenery, apparently in a very similar manner,
would be an interesting subject of discussion. In
elaborate and loving treatment of landscape, however,
the Flemish painters distinctly led the way. The
veracity which held them so firmly to the stern

delineation of the thing which they saw in the human face, taught them likewise to look with humility upon the face of nature, and to be content to imitate her in a spirit of like conscientiousness. The earliest known picture of the van Eycks, the altar-piece of the 'Adoration of the Lamb,' is in this respect perhaps as far advanced as anything afterwards produced. Later painters learned to treat natural scenes more broadly, and to imitate a wider scale of natural phenomena, but nothing that they made is more perfect of its kind than the gardens of Paradise in the picture referred to.

An historical discussion of the landscape work of this school will find place further on, but in the present connection it cannot be out of place to dwell briefly upon its leading virtue of veracity. Of course veracity in landscape art may be of several kinds. A painter may reproduce with perfect truth the general effect produced upon him by a scene. A precipice may be imposing in his eyes by reason of its height, and may render, for the time, in his imagination, all surrounding objects mean in comparison. If in his picture the precipice be more lofty than trigonometrical measurements would allow, he nevertheless need lie under no accusation of unfaithfulness. He has actually reproduced an effect of truth. Moreover, the complexity of nature being so infinite, so utterly beyond the power of eye and mind to comprehend, and still more impossible for the hand to reproduce in all its infinity of detail, an artist, however conscientious, must omit much, nay must omit far more than he introduces. It thus becomes interesting to observe, in every case, what are the objects chosen by a landscape painter out of the infinity before him, and what are the objects refused. Now in Flemish landscapes the chief features are always much the same — clear blue skies lightly flecked with clouds of tenderest white, undulating hills, gently-flowing streams, country roads winding amongst green trees, little hamlets or walled towns or monastic buildings all breathing an air of quiet and peace. In fact it is the domestic scenery of the Maas valley that we behold, and we have every reason to believe that the scenes represented are actual views of localities known to the contemporary spectator. In the treatment of buildings the artist allows himself a certain amount of latitude, and often alters the architectural details to accord with his own taste. Now and again, in the abrupter hill slopes, we notice the introduction of an emphasis personal to the artist; but such slight changes are of trifling importance. In all else the most rigid adherence to nature and fact is the inviolable rule with these earnest men. And it is especially with the small things of nature that this veracity becomes most apparent. They cannot cover the whole of

I

their foregrounds with a carpet of flowers, painted in finished elaboration ; they were forced, therefore, to sacrifice either the quantity or the finish of these floral jewels. They did not hesitate a moment, but, abandoning the method which would have dotted the grass with spots of various tints, and so suggested one side of the truth, they set themselves to reproduce with absolute accuracy a few representative and symbolic flowers, and left them, as an arabesque on a background of green, for a memorial of their countless fellows, fair as they. In the rendering of foliage a like difficulty encountered them, and they overcame it in a similar way. It was impossible to outline and colour each individual leaf, even of those that the eye could clearly distinguish. Here again, then, they might mass the foliage together, and, avoiding all detail, paint the masses truly as far as truth was possible, or they might depict accurately a few individual leaves, charging them, like the flowers, with a representative function. Their love of minute veracity made them choose, and for a long time adhere to, the latter laborious alternative.

Veracity of this kind was of the essence of all the work produced by the school under consideration ; it was the natural quality of a set of men whose ideal possessed the character above described. They could not tolerate anything short of close approximation to truth. They could not withhold their hand so long as aught of incompleteness or inexactitude remained which it was in their power to remove. Thus in portrait they carried the delineation of a face to a point of a finish such as artists of no other school (except Leonardo da Vinci) ever attained. They were not to be satisfied with a picture which suggested in general fashion the likeness of a man ; they insisted upon working out to the uttermost every little shade of expression. The dimpled foldings of the lips were not enough for them ; they would pursue the traces of a smile to the very extremities of the visage. It was the same in their treatment of every part. The smallest wrinkles of the hand the least peculiarity in the form of a finger-nail or an ear, did not escape their notice. They wrought the garments with like painstaking. Textures and patterns of richest or commonest substances were reproduced with faithful veracity; jewelled hems, clasps, and trinkets, were designed with the full knowledge of a goldsmith versed in his craft. The very hairs of the head were almost painted one by one. No artist in fact could have succeeded in that day unless he were a man of wonderful diligence. And this was but natural. The Flemish painter worked for a race of men more industrious probably than any others the world has seen. His employers knew, each in his own sphere, what good workmanship was like, and they could not be satisfied with

I 2

art of a slovenly character. By a natural process of evolution, therefore, the art-schools of mediæval Flanders produced a set of painters of persevering tenacity such as have nowhere else appeared, except perhaps in Venice and Franconia, under similar conditions.

Owing to the nature of the climate these laborious and painstaking artists were obliged to spend the best part of their energies, not, as in Italy, in the frescoing of walls, but in painting upon panels. The method of painting employed in the fourteenth century had been what is known as *tempera*. The ground-work of the panel was prepared with a coating of fine plaster, called *gesso*, and upon this the colours were laid by help of a medium such as white of egg or the juice of unripe figs. Oil was likewise used as a medium even from very early days,* but its use was attended with great disadvantages. It was difficult to lay the colours finely with it, and then they took a long time to dry. Hence oil was never used in the finished parts of the work, but only for masses of drapery and the like. As the demand for fine works of art increased, and the skill of painters developed, they longed, we cannot doubt, to discover some method of painting by means of which they might be enabled to produce more delicately finished and

* A Louvain painter of the fourteenth century was nicknamed John Oilpot.

more enduring works. For another great objection to the old *tempora* method, as far as northern countries are concerned, was that they suffered rapid deterioration from damp. In Westminster Abbey there is an old retable, painted in this manner. The colours have flaked off it in large patches, and left the panels bare over the greater part of the surface. Such, no doubt, was the fate of most of the works of fourteenth century painting in the Low Countries ; and so we are scarcely possessed of any but the most meagre materials for forming an estimate of it. Now, artists of the kind that we know these Flemings to have been, lavish of their labour and unfaltering in their care, were just the men to whom this destruction of their labour would be intolerable. No one is willing that a work which has drunk his life-blood for months should quickly perish. For the full development, therefore, of an art, such as the Low Countries were capable of producing, a great improvement in the method of painting was requisite, and that improvement must be such as to make finer work possible, and to give greater durability to its completed results.

We may well assume, though materials are lacking for support of the assumption, that artists set them-selves with characteristic industry to find satisfaction for the need they experienced. Of those who sought and failed, however, we know nothing, but only of those who succeeded in the quest—the brothers Hubert and Jan van Eyck. They are usually credited, since the days of Vasari and Van Mander, with the discovery of what we call oil-painting. But this is not true. Oil, as we have seen, was used as a vehicle long before their day. On the other hand, oil-painting of the kind to which we are accustomed was not invented by them, or indeed by any one, but arose out of a long process of development, in which they did indeed contribute an important step, but which had been advancing before they were born, and continued to advance after they had been long dead and buried.

The real point of the invention of the Van Eycks seems to have been the discovery of a substance, which, when mixed with boiled oil, caused it to dry rapidly without the necessity of exposure to the sun. This substance was probably resin. Hubert and Jan were not men to rest content with any slight advance, so for years they seem to have worked at perfecting the new process, and eventually they became complete masters of its utmost refinements. None of their followers, for a century, surpassed them as craftsmen, altogether apart from any question of the artistic quality of their work.

So far as we can judge by examining pictures of the school, the method of painting was somewhat as follows. The panel was planed smooth, and then covered, as for the old *tempera* process, with a coating

of *gesso.* The design was next drawn with perfect
exactitude upon the white surface, and the broad
masses of colour were laid on. All the details of the
work, all the fine lights and elaborate modelling, were
superimposed upon the ground tones by means of
colour mixed with a transparent varnish, and the whole
was wrought so finely together that at last the surface
became like enamel, and it is generally next to impossible to discover the traces of the brush. This
method, it will be observed, is different from that now
called oil-painting, in which the colours are laid on by
aid of a medium of an oily character, and when the
picture is finished, the whole surface is protected by
a final transparent coating of varnish. In Flemish
pictures the varnish was incorporated with the surface
colours, and cannot be removed without destroying
at the same time the very fabric of the work. For
this reason all attempts to, what is called, *restore,* or
clean pictures of the Flemish school, result only in
the destruction of the work, and by this means many
fine pictures have, for all practical purposes, perished.
A Madonna in the National Gallery, ascribed to Memling, is a lamentable example of this kind of ruin.
The method of the Van Eycks was a half-way stage
between those of the old *tempera* painters and of
modern artists. It still retained the *gesso* ground
and the panel, whilst it involved the use of varnishes.
A century later the change was carried to completion

in the studios of Venice under the hands of Titian and his fellows. For their rapid style of work the Flemish system was not suited. It was fitted alone for men of the same stamp as its discoverers—men willing to devote hours to the patient elaboration of a detail, and who considered their lives well invested, if at the end they left behind them a moderate number of small but excellently finished jewels.

We may now proceed, in conclusion, to consider how this method, of their devising, reacted upon the painters of the Flemish school. It was of a kind only applicable to work on a small scale ; it permitted such work to be brought to an astonishing degree of finish by expenditure of sufficient labour. There do indeed exist a few large pictures of the school, not-ably the Ghent altar-piece by the Van Eycks, the 'Last Judgment,' at Beaune, by Roger van der Weyden, and the 'Nativity,' at Florence, by Hugo van der Goes. But of these the first two are only assemblages of smaller panels framed together, their subjects being related more or less closely one to another, whilst Hugo's picture by no means gains in attractiveness in proportion to its size, but would have looked more beautiful had it been smaller and better finished throughout, after the usual manner of the school.

An artist is of necessity led to expend upon pictures which are small and laboriously wrought an amount of care in the design, and especially in the quality of the colours, by no means so imperative in larger works. Such a painting as the 'Last Judgment' by Tintoret in the Doge's Palace at Venice produces some impression upon the most casual spectator by means of its size alone. Details are not considered, and even the harmony of colour becomes less imperative when the field of vision is unable to contain the whole area of the canvas at once. But the eye takes in at a glance the whole of one of these tiny pictures of the Flemish school, and if the colouring is poor in quality, or faulty in combination, the defect is immediately apparent. Every charm that can be bestowed upon so small a surface is requisite to intensify its attractive power; and hence Flemish painters, aided by their new-found method, developed a jewel-like quality of colouring which remained peculiar to themselves. The especial love of jewellery manifested at that time by the wealthy of the Low Countries, and the consequent taste and skill acquired by the goldsmiths of the day, may not have been without influence in this respect. That this love of jewels was shared by the painters is sufficiently shown by the amount and beauty of the jewelled ornaments introduced by them into their pictures. Not only are brooches and clasps, sceptres and crowns, studded with precious stones, but the hems of garments are continually sewn with them, whilst gloves and shoes of state are likewise so adorned.

It was further natural that when figures had to be painted on so small a scale the artist should prefer to clothe them in stuffs of great magnificence. And here again the fashion of the time and the necessary tendency of its art were in accord. No mediæval or modern court, not even that of Paris in the days of the Second Empire, can have compared for magnificence of outward apparel with the court of the Dukes of Burgundy in the fifteenth century. Flanders was alike the centre of weaving and of Oriental commerce. The silks of the East were unloaded upon her quays, and sold in all the markets of the land; at the same time the looms of Arras, Brussels, and Ghent vied with one another in the richness and beauty of their productions. Thus the painters of the Low Countries were made constantly familiar with all manner of rich stuffs, and they were eager to show in their works the splendid results of their experience. Even in the least excellent pictures by nameless pupils of the school, the stuffs are usually well and richly painted, and so are all those accessories of jewel and flower, which admitted of being reproduced by any workman well taught in the methods of his craft, and willing to expend the requisite amount of pains.

In the Flemish style, as we have said, it was impossible to paint large or fast. An artist had to plan his picture thoroughly beforehand, and to know exactly what he was going to do. After the *gesso* ground had been prepared, the picture drawn in, and its undertones laid on, it was almost impossible to alter anything except details, and it was hard to lay aside what had already cost so much time. Painters like Titian, whose pictures from beginning to end seldom took him as many days as those of a Fleming occupied months, might, with little sacrifice, abandon any unpromising work and start afresh. They were thus induced to make many new ventures, and to design with originality. Northern artists experienced no such encouragement; on the contrary, the tendency with them was, of necessity, the other way. The series of subjects, portraits apart, which they were called upon to depict, were relatively few in number, and showed little indication of increasing. For each subject, typical methods of treatment became habitual, and artists and patrons alike preferred to adhere to them, with moderate constancy, rather than to strive for an originality which might well be accompanied by a smaller measure of success. Memling almost always painted pictures of the enthroned Virgin with Saints according to one design, particular saints being introduced as the circumstances of the case required, or if none were wanted, then angels took their place.

Thus the chief qualities of the Flemish school may be called Veracity of Imitation, Jewel-like richness of

Colour, perfection of Finish, emphasis of Character, and Conservatism in design. These indeed are virtues enough to make a school of art great in the annals of time, even though they may never be able to win for it the clatter of popular applause. The paintings of Flanders were not, and were not intended to be, popular. Flemish artists did not, like the Italians, paint for the folk, but for the delight of a small clique of cultured and solid individuals. They painted as their employers worked, with energy, honesty, and endurance ; they cared not for beauty of the more palpable and less enduring kind, but they cared infinitely for Truth ; for her they laboured in humility, satisfied with the joy of their own obedience, and then, when they slept and knew not of it, she came and clothed the children of their industry with her own unfading garments of loveliness and life.

CHAPTER IV.

THE VAN EYCKS.

ST. PAUL, in a moment of fine enthusiasm, declared that the single virtue of charity is superior to all others, so that without it they profit nothing. We, looking back upon what generations have left behind them of labour crystallized into form, and noting how often men of splendid endowments but little tenacity have passed away into forgetfulness, like a gay ripple across a sun-lit sea, might be tempted to believe that for the artist there is a different virtue absolutely essential, and that that virtue is Industry. Now and again, perhaps, some extraordinary genius has arisen, to whom success seems to have come without effort on his part ; but either the appearance is illusory, or else the man was born in a happy hour and reaped the reward, for which the soil was tilled and the seed sown, by the faithful labours of his less remembered forefathers. But the nobler measure of praise belongs to one finely endowed by nature, who patiently continues from day to day improving the gifts and enlarging the powers which have been rendered into his stewardship. And assuredly the spirit of him who gazes will be more kindled and exalted by watching the strong and steady winging towards its aim of a keen-sighted and experienced mind, than the sudden and impetuous rocket-flight of a wild imagination, accompanied though it be by never so many brilliant coruscations and startling surprises.

Amongst artists few have been more gifted and none more earnest than the two with whom the early Flemish school culminated. It is not true that the brothers Van Eyck were the founders of that school. There were many and excellent painters in the Low Countries before their day, as the few surviving works and the ancient records testify. The Van Eycks introduced great changes, and may be said to have originated a new style, which became so popular that pictures of the old school went out of fashion and were replaced by others more in accordance with the new taste ; but the brothers must nevertheless be considered rather as the culminating than the founding artists of the school. Fourteenth century Flemish pictures are indeed rare ; but there remain a few excellent wall-paintings, and meritorious panel-pictures are likewise discoverable, as for instance at Dijon. All this pre-Van Eyck Flemish work is of the style of the Rhenish school, and closely resembles the work of the Köln painters. Indeed, ancient records seem to show that most of the artists who worked in Flanders in the fourteenth century and the early years of the fifteenth were Germans, following the traditions of Meister Wilhelm and the mystic school. The mild enthusiasm and purity of heart which characterized the early mystics, degenerated at the commencement of the fifteenth century into a mawkish sentimentality. This kind of thing was not likely long to suit the taste of the common-sense burghers of phlegmatic Flanders, and, if art was ever to be a living thing for them and not a mere toy, a new spirit must be breathed into it, and they must do that for themselves. The change which took place under the Van Eycks and their followers was thus in great part due to the new nationality of the artists. It was the result of a transference of art from German to Dutch and Flemish hands. Just such a change took place also in commercial Venice. The Venetians, busy with their trade, preferred for a long time to buy, rather than to produce, the works of art they required. The time, however, came when their ideals and needs were different from those of any other people, and the difference lay in a superior robustness. Then they had to settle down and make works of art for themselves, and in a few years they produced a school as powerful as any in the world.

Without breaking with the past the Flemish painters of the fifteenth century introduced a new spirit into the old work, and while they modified the ideal, they modified also the technical method of working.

It is one of our greatest misfortunes, as students of the history of art, that none of the early works of the brothers Hubert and Jan Van Eyck exist to our knowledge. Hubert was born at Maaseyck (near Maastricht) about the year 1366, Jan was born about 1380, and is traditionally asserted to have been brought up by his elder brother. At some time or another they removed to Ghent, where, in the year 1421, they were admitted into the Painters' Guild. Jan went off for a couple of years to the Hague, whilst Hubert remained behind earning a high reputation. About the year 1424 he received an order for a great altar-piece, but in 1426, before he had done much more than make a commencement upon it, the swift hand of death bore him away, and the work was left to Jan to be carried out. This picture, the world-renowned ' Adoration of the Lamb,' at St. Bavon's Church in Ghent, is the only example we possess of Hubert's handiwork, and the earliest specimen of Jan's. It is painted in the improved manner invented by one or the other of the brothers, or by both conjointly. We have thus no indications of what Hubert's early work was like, either as to its ideal or its method. We are unable to trace the growth of his mind or of the invention he made, and we do not know to which of the two brothers the greatest credit is due. Suddenly the old ideal and the old methods seem to be supplanted by this improved method and wholly changed ideal. In all the history of art there exists no such other gap.

The 'Adoration of the Lamb'* is thus a monumental work of unique importance. It is unfortunate that, owing to the greed or indifference of some churchmen, its wings have been dismembered from the centre-piece and distributed in part to Brussels and in part to Berlin, their place at Ghent being taken by feeble copies.

On the outsides of the wings there is an Annunciation in the upper four panels, the scene being laid in the painter's own studio, with a view out of the windows looking over the town of Ghent. In the four panels below are Jodocus Vijts and his wife, who paid for the picture, and by their sides two images of their patron saints.

It is, however, to the interior when the wings are opened that attention will be chiefly directed. The picture is an illustration of the following passages from St. John's Apocalypse: "I looked, and, lo, a Lamb stood on the mount Sion, and with Him an hundred and forty and four thousand, having His

---

* The Arundel Society has published a reproduction of it with an imitation of the original frame.

K

Father's name written in their foreheads. And I
heard a voice from heaven, as the voice of many
waters, and as the voice of a great thunder: and I
heard the voice of harpers harping with their harps:
and they sung as it were a new song before the
throne, and before the four beasts, and the elders:
and no man could learn that song but the hundred
and forty and four thousand, which were redeemed
from the earth . . . . These are they which follow
the Lamb whithersoever he goeth. These were redeemed from among men, being the first-fruits unto
God and to the Lamb. And in their mouth was
found no guile: for they are without fault before the
throne of God." And again, "I beheld, and, lo, a
great multitude, which no man could number, clothed
with white robes, and palms in their hands . . . .
These are they which came out of great tribulation,
and have washed their robes, and made them white
in the blood of the Lamb. Therefore are they before
the throne of God ; and He shall feed them, and shall
lead them to living fountains of waters, and shall wipe
away all tears from their eyes."

Upon the principal panel in the centre below is the
Adoration of the Lamb ; on the lower panels of the
wings on either side of it are the Just Judges and
the Knights, the Saints and the Hermits advancing
to adore. The noble figure of Christ, King of
Heaven, seated between the Virgin and John Baptist

(as he is usually represented in pictures of the Last Judgment), occupies the upper central portion, whilst in the corresponding parts of the wings on either side are choirs of playing and singing angels, and Adam and Eve representing. the fallen, as the Virgin and John the redeemed, human race.

Tradition asserts with probable correctness that two of the Just Judges are portraits of Hubert and Jan van Eyck. Hubert is the man in front on the white horse; Jan with the mild face and lurking smile is somewhat behind, dressed in black. The same two persons appear in another picture ascribed to Van Eyck, the 'Fountain of Life' at Madrid, to which reference will presently be made. Amongst the Knights are St. Michael and St. George, St. Maurice and Kaiser Karl. Knights and Judges together represent the two sides of the active life. The hermits and pilgrims, devoted to a life of contemplation, are opposed to them on the other wing. All four parties move along tortuous ways through a beautiful country towards the mystic altar of the Lamb. The nearer they approach, the more richly is the country wooded, and the clearer and purer is the over-arching sky. About the altar itself on every side flowers burst into joyful bloom—violets and pansies, cowslips, daisies, and lilies of the valley all in their fairest colours. Behind are purple flags, lilies, roses, and vines in fullest strength of life

K 2

and glow of blossom; no stricken bud, no blighted
leaf, no withered flower amongst them all, for they
grow in the soil of Paradise, where there is no decay.
Even the stones in the brook are jewels, and the
water of life washes them.

Those who have already arrived are grouped in
adoration on either side of the altar. Ranged in
front are the apostles, fourteen in number, including
Paul and Mathias; behind are Popes, Bishops, and
a body of the faithful. Over against them are the
ancient prophets, those of the Jews in front, those of
the Gentiles (including Homer, Plato, and Aristotle)
ranked behind, all alike inspired by the rays of
spiritual illumination which fall from the hovering
Dove.

The fountain of life is placed in front, and the water
of it flows through the ages along its jewelled bed.

Behind, amongst the rose bushes, are the holy
martyrs with palm branches in their hands; amongst
the lilies opposite to them are the martyred virgins
led by Barbera, Agnes, Catherine, and Dorothy.

Angels with gorgeous rainbow-coloured wings kneel
round about the altar, some in contemplation holding
the instruments of the Passion, some in adoration
gazing on the emblem of Divine love, some swinging
their censers, the symbols of prayer, till they touch
the words embroidered in letters of gold, "Jesus the
Way, the Truth, and the Life." As the key-note to

the whole composition the painter has written, along the front of the altar, this text from his Latin Testament: "Behold the Lamb of God, that taketh away the sins of the world."

Finer even than this is the upper portion of the middle picture, generally admitted to be the work of Hubert, as the Adoration panel is certainly the work of Jan. The figure of Christ, the King of heaven, is one of the grandest creations of all art, and can be paralleled only by the head of Christ in Dürer's picture of the 'Adoration of all Saints,' now at Vienna. "Here eyes do regard you from Eternity's *stillness*," says Goethe. Majestic calm is the leading quality in this face. In the forehead is intellectual power ; the eyes are mild yet deep as the ocean, the hand is full of strength, the pose of the figure is greatly dignified. The word *Sabaoth* is embroidered on the hem of His robe, the diadem of glory and the triple crown of heavenly law are upon His head ; in His hand is the sceptre of irrefrangible command, at His feet lies the crown of earthly rule. "Heaven is His throne, earth is His footstool." As contrast and commentary there is embroidered again and again, on the curtain behind, the symbol of charity and self-sacrifice, the Pelican nourishing her young with flesh plucked from her own breast, and beneath it the name "Ihesus Christus." Along the front of the dais, whereon His feet are placed, are these words

written : "In His head life without death, on His
forehead youth without age, joy without sorrow on
His right hand, security without fear on His left."

Scarcely less beautiful is the figure of the Virgin,
the representative of all glorified women, as John
Baptist of all glorified men. Specially interesting is
the symbolism of her crown. The hair represents
always the strength of life, and the crown the obedience to Divine law that governs and restrains it.
The Nazarite, who devoted himself to the Lord, let
his hair grow in token that his life was no longer his
own, to order it according to his pleasure. The
Pagan cast a lock of his hair into the sacred river of
his land, or burnt it to his god in the sacrificial fire, as
a sign of his self-dedication. The fillet, therefore, that
binds the hair symbolizes the obedience to eternal
law which binds the life ; and so the crown primarily
symbolizes obedience, and only secondarily command,
because he alone is fit to order others who himself
has learnt to obey. "He that ruleth over men must
be just, ruling in the fear of God ; and he shall be
as the light of morning when the sun ariseth, even
a morning without cloud ; as the tender grass spring-
ing out of the earth by clear shining after rain." The
crown of thorns is the parent of all others, and they,
like it, alone become glorious by obedient wearing,
even as the rod of martyrdom is changed into the
martyr's palm.

The most beautiful virtue of the Virgin, to the mediæval mind, was her humility, and the symbol of that was the lily of the valley. "The Lord hath regarded the lowliness of His handmaiden." Her crown is a crown of lowliness, a ring of wild and humble flowers—the lily of the valley, the wild rose, and the rod lily. But she wore it in patient and meek obedience, and so she could thereafter sing, "He that is mighty hath magnified me, and Holy is His name; behold, from henceforth all generations shall call me Blessed." And so in sign of her great reward the binding fillet of lowly obedience glitters with rubies and topaz and pearls; the humble flowers toss themselves up in their joy, and are strong with unfading vigour; the lilies and the hare-bells hold up their heads in the fulness of a larger life; the petals of the wild roses glow with richer tones. And above the blossoms glitter their brothers of the night, a sevenfold coronal of stars. The crown of humility has become a crown of glory too.

The work of painting this picture occupied eight years, for it was ordered in 1424, and not completed till May 1432. The inscription placed upon it states that "Hubert van Eyck, than whom none greater has appeared, began the work, which Jan his brother, in art the second, brought to completion." How much of the whole design was prepared by Hubert, and how much of the actual painting was done by his hand, we cannot for certain say. After Hubert's death Jan did not at once set to work on it, for he was resident then at Lille, in the service of Philip the Good, Duke of Burgundy, and was by him several times sent on mysterious missions, probably to paint the portraits of ladies, the Duke being at that time on the look-out for a wife. In the winter of 1428-29 he was sent on such a mission to Portugal, to make the portrait of Princess Isabella. On his return he settled down permanently at Bruges, and there no doubt in the years 1429 to 1432 the great Ghent altar-piece was finished.

The only other existing picture of the school at all like the 'Adoration of the Lamb' is the 'Fountain of Living Water' at Madrid. Some critics have ascribed it to Hubert, others consider it to be a sixteenth-century copy of a lost work by Hubert or John. Whether original or copy, it at all events preserves for us a composition of great importance. The scene upon which the figures are ranged is divided into three stages. On the upper stage Christ is seated in majesty upon a throne under a great canopy, with the Virgin and John the Evangelist by His side. Upon the middle stage are playing and singing angels, whilst upon the lower is the fountain of living water, by which the Pope, the Emperor, and other representatives of the organized body of Christendom are reverently kneeling on the one side,

ADAM

EVA

CK.

To face p. 136.

whilst representatives of the old Jewish religion are grouped on the other side in consternation and despair. The throne of Christ is adorned with sculptured figures of prophets and of the beasts symbolic of the four evangelists. At His feet lies the Lamb of God, and just below it the pure river of water of life, clear as crystal, proceeds out of the throne of God and of the Lamb, and bears along holy wafers of spiritual food, through the fountain, which is the Catholic Church, to the hungry and thirsty world.

The symbolism of the picture is sufficiently plain, but it is graceless and forced. The same to a less degree is the case in the 'Adoration of the Lamb.' Symbolism is a language capable of expressing many things which speech cannot well convey. By a symbol a man's thoughts may be directed towards things out of any artist's power to represent or poet's to describe. Such a symbol was the Lamb of God. Mediæval sculptors and painters never represented the lamb as a mere animal. They always made it carry a banner, emblematic of the resurrection ; they treated it, moreover, in a decorative fashion—carved it alone as a boss or on a key-stone, not as the centre-piece of a group of human figures. Thus, if you understand what the Lamb meant to the mediæval mind, your thoughts when you see it are directed along a certain channel. If you do not understand anything about its meaning, it is still an object

decoratively treated. In the Ghent altar-piece, on
the contrary, the symbolic creature is painted with
perfect realistic veracity. It does not look like a
symbol, it looks like a sheep; and instead of at once
suggesting a mystic thought, it shocks the eye by its
sturdy realism, and that all the more strongly because
it is not even an adjunct (as in the 'Fountain of
Life'), but the central object of the whole picture.

Veracity, we have seen, was the key-note of Flemish
art, and that particular virtue is more clearly manifested in the work of Jan van Eyck than in that of
any of his followers. Of all Flemish painters he was
the most emphatically national, and independent of
external influences. The national character attained
its highest development and its noblest expression
in and through him. Now this very virtue of perfect
veracity is inconsistent with the use of symbolic
methods in art. Ideal characters, ideal conceptions,
do not belong to a painter like Jan van Eyck. His
peculiar power lay in keen penetration into actual
fact. Thus in the Madrid picture he has to show
that Christians are invigorated and comforted by the
life of Christ, and that Jews are disturbed and con-
founded at it. He therefore represents a company
of Christian dignitaries kneeling on the one hand in
reverent satisfaction; whilst on the other hand, for
no apparent cause, the Jews tear their garments,
and the high priest, representing the synagogue, his

eyes blinded with a handkerchief, falls backwards as stricken by a blow, the pole of the standard in his hand being at the same moment shattered in pieces. All this is done without the visible interference of any agency, no encouraging angel on the one side, or indignant angel on the other. It is not as though the Pope and high priest had been mere emblematic figures, such as we find sculptured on the outside of many a Gothic cathedral, or painted by Jan van Eyck himself among the sculptured ornaments of the Madonna's canopy in the beautiful little picture * belonging to Mr. Beresford Hope. Here they are actual human beings, portraits executed with marvellous fidelity and insight into individual character. It is just that fidelity and insight which destroyed the old thirteenth and fourteenth century art of fantasy and faith, and produced the fifteenth-century school of actual fact. A further proof of Jan's lack of understanding of the old ideals may be drawn from a consideration of the individual figures in the Madrid picture. The Christ is no longer the dignified and majestic King which Hubert made Him, but a person of insignificant and almost anxious mien. The Virgin is a sweet woman, the angels chubby and smiling children. But, beyond question, the finest part of the whole is the group of leaders of Christendom, in which every face is a portrait full of power and vigour,

* Phot. South Kensington Museum.

and executed with a masculine veracity. Specially fine is the profile of the Emperor, whilst the portraits of Hubert kneeling conspicuously in the foreground, and of Jan standing up behind, are of great value for comparison with those on the wing of the Ghent altar-piece.

The individual character of a great artist and the general tendency of his day are always in perfect harmony, because the thing which makes an artist great is the clearness and precision with which he gives form to the ideals of his contemporaries. Activity and enterprise were the leading qualities of the Flemish in Jan van Eyck's day. Industry was full of vigour, men were growing rich, and at the same time increasing in their knowledge of the actual world wherein they lived. A new continent was shortly to be discovered, trade routes were being changed. In every direction the world of nature tended to win for itself much of the attention which previous generations had devoted to the world of spirit. When, therefore, we turn away from Jan van Eyck's ideal pictures to those in which the portrait element had freer play, we are leaving a group of subjects of yearly decreasing interest to the men of Flanders, and we are approaching a field of art in which they found continually greater delight.

Comparing Jan's Madonnas with those of his predecessors and contemporaries a little way up the valley of the Rhine, we find a notable difference. Excepting only the Virgin of the Annunciation now in the Hermitage at St. Petersburg, they are always self-possessed and in a very composed frame of mind. They give no evidence of spiritual exaltation, and the same may be said of Jan's saints. Even St. Francis receiving in an ecstacy the sacred wounds of Christ upon his own body, a picture recently discovered on the walls of the Turin Gallery,*—even St. Francis, whose legend was well known to every Christian in Europe in Van Eyck's day, and who was the very incarnation of extravagant mysticism, when Jan depicts him at the culminating moment of a life of visions and dreams, appears as a stout and well-conditioned Fleming, reverent and thoughtful indeed, but thoroughly composed of mind. Moreover, neither the Virgin nor any of the saints possess the dignity of bearing suited to the Queen and aristocracy of heaven. They are indeed dressed in the rich costumes fashionable among the great people at the Court of the Dukes of Burgundy, the most sumptuous Court in Europe at that time, but their faces are plain, and their expressions often familiar. Take for example the Madonna with St. George and St. Donatian now in the Academy at Bruges. St. George is in the act of introducing his

* Phot. Brogi of Florence. Lord Heytesbury's picture is a smaller replica of this. Some think it a copy.

ponderous protégé, Canon George de Pala, to the enthroned Virgin and Child. As he does so he makes a bow and takes off his hat, smiling—we might almost say grinning—at the seemingly frightened Child. (See wood cut, p. 99.)

For this want of sublimity in Jan's art there is ample compensation in the new qualities with which his fearless veracity so richly endowed it. He has, for instance, to paint a portrait of St. Barbera, as in the unfinished panel in the Museum at Antwerp. He takes her legend literally, and depicts it according to the circumstances of his own day with simple truth.

The legend runs that Barbera's father shut her up in a tower, fearful lest her marvellous beauty should attract suitors to her, and that so he should lose his only child. In her tower she, being a lady of great intellect, gave herself up to meditation and study, and came to the conclusion that the God who made the stars of heaven could be none of those whom her father worshipped. The rest of the tale is immaterial to us now; suffice it to say that she became a Christian, and suffered martyrdom. Jan van Eyck represents her as a fair young Flemish maiden (holding for form's sake a martyr's palm) seated out of doors upon the ground reading in a book. In the background a multitude of workmen are building such a tower as Jan thought would be suitable for

so fine a princess. It is the best thing in the way of
a decorated Gothic tower he could devise. He drew
it with literal accuracy—the crane on the top hoisting

ST. BARBERA. BY JAN VAN EYCK. *Antwerp Museum.*

up the stones, the workmen labouring at their various
tasks, some wheeling up the rough blocks upon
barrows, some cutting and squaring them under a
mason's shed, some fitting them into their places.

It is the truest representation of the actual way
building operations were carried on in the fifteenth
and preceding centuries. No doubt if you take what
St. Barbera was to the mystic mediæval mind,
namely, the saintly representative of the contemplative life, you do not find her depicted by Jan van
Eyck ; but if you regard the name of the picture as
nothing more than a name, you will find that the
work itself contains qualities of the highest artistic
merit, besides being a historic record of lasting
human interest.

In Mr. Beresford Hope's Madonna standing under
a canopy, symbolic of the gate of heaven, though the
symbolism is more finely carried out than in any
other of Van Eyck's pictures, the chief interest lies
neither in it nor yet in the divinity of the persons
represented, but rather in their complete humanity.
Apart from the mere æsthetic pleasure which the eye
derives from the harmony of colours, the play of light,
and the rich combination of textures, a pleasure
which all the master's works afford without exception,
the picture depends solely upon the human relation
between the Mother and Child for its charm. That
she is the Blessed Virgin Mary and that He is the
holy Child Jesus in no way adds to or detracts from
the idea of the picture. The essential fact which it
bears on the face of it, and beyond which the painter
does not attempt to penetrate, is that she is a loving

mother and He a frolicsome babe.* The human
interest is supreme, and it raises the art to a level
from which it addresses not merely a set of people
of a certain religion, but all men and women of every
epoch. So long as mothers and babies exist this
picture will speak to them in a manner which cannot
be misunderstood.

Thus Jan van Eyck, in losing touch of the religious
idea, in no way lowered his art, but on the contrary
raised it. Reverence, the grand fundamental spirit of
all true religions, was as strong, nay stronger, in him
than in his mystic predecessors ; only his reverence
was for incarnate spirits visibly around him, and for
the material earth and heavens that shut him in from
the infinities on every side. The supreme virtue in his
pictures is, therefore, the expression of reverent study
of the two great things perennially interesting—Man
and Nature. Religious systems of thought, systems

* The Berlin Gallery possesses, amongst other genuine works
by Jan van Eyck, a little picture of the Virgin standing, in the
nave of the church of the Abbey of the Dunes (525 C.). There
is a copy of this at Antwerp forming part of a diptych dated 1499,
and painted by some follower of Memling. The other half of
the diptych bears a portrait of the donor, John le Clerc, Abbot
of the Dunes. In the library of the University of Cambridge is
a MS. written for this same Abbot, and likewise adorned with
his monogram, coat-of-arms, and portrait. The Virgin in the
Berlin picture is represented as of colossal size, and gorgeously
clothed and crowned, but in all other respects she is just a
Flemish woman of the middle-class, looking strangely unsuited
to such attire.

L

of society, come and go, but the human interest
abides, and the image of a once actually living
man is of everlasting value. For this reason the
highest kind of portraiture is the highest kind of
art. Photography can render the features of a man,
but it can seldom, if ever, produce a portrait of
him. For a true portrait is the image of a man thinking. The flesh is but the expression of the mind.
Like the mind, it is partly moulded by heredity, but
far more by actions done and thoughts felt. A smile
that recurs often leaves at length permanent traces, a
frequent frown bends the brows even in slumber.
Yet no expression returns again exactly the same,
and no face is any less variable than the sky of
heaven, which the moving sun and the changing
clouds every moment alter with infinite variety. Like
the landscape painter, the painter of portraits has to
choose his moment and to catch his subject at its
best. He has by long observation to see and fix in
his memory those almost imperceptible tremblings
of the eye and twitchings of the lips wherein the character of the subject manifests itself. Thus the great
virtues of a painter of portraits are swiftness to
observe, tenacity to remember, and veracity to depict,
and all these virtues Jan van Eyck possessed to a
remarkable degree. Different men make different
uses of the same qualities, according to their other
characteristics, and according to the standard of the

day in which they live. Reynolds dashed off a thousand or more portraits in the course of half a century, and every one of them catches with greater or less insight and veracity the character of the person depicted. But as a rule Reynolds does not plunge deep into the character; he gives you the general outlines of it as he does of the face. The people of his day wanted to be painted fast. Van Eyck, on the contrary, painted very few pictures, but those he finished with an industry almost unique. Nature will beat any artist in finish. Magnify one of her details a thousand diameters, and draw all you can see, you will be no nearer completeness, for it might be magnified a thousand times more and the details would not only be magnified but multiplied a thousandfold. Moreover, an artist, even the most patient, has neither the time nor the skill to set down all he can see. He has to omit the greater part. Dürer says that if he were to finish one of the small heads, in a picture upon which he was at work, up to the point to which he could carry it, that alone would take him six months. Jan van Eyck never left a thing less complete than his powers availed to make it. The motto that he chose proves this : "As I can, not as I wish." His pictures show that every touch was a work of love. He worked on and on at the surface glazings till every sign of roughness disappeared. The very elaborateness of the technique hides the

individual traces of the brush. The surface is like
enamel, and even a magnifying glass will seldom
reveal an imperfection. To us it seems a high price
for a man to pay for his fame; but mark the result.
Jan van Eyck's pictures have lasted without sensible
deterioration, even when they have been but poorly
cared for. They have always been prized and must
always be worthy of prizing; the works of other less
industrious men have fallen to pieces or greatly deteriorated, and most of them have passed through long
epochs of neglect. The honest hard work of John
van Eyck has made his pictures perennially delightful.

The National Gallery is fortunate in possessing
three of the finest specimens of Jan's portraiture.*
One is the picture of John Arnolfini and his wife
standing in their bedroom; another is the charming
" Leal Souvenir" of a man who doubtless was the
painter's friend; the third, and in some respects the
best, is the portrait of an unknown person, wearing
a red turban. There is a peculiar simplicity in Jan
van Eyck's character; everything that he does
exactly fits in with our first idea of him. He is not
like so many who do contradictory things which are
not easy to reconcile. He is always direct, always
the same; every insight he gives us into himself
shows the same simplicity and serenity of heart.
The very inscriptions he puts on his pictures are

* Photo. Braun and Berlin Phot. Company.

thus characteristic. The portrait of the Arnolfini is signed, "Jan van Eyck was here." He only professed to come, look, and record what he saw. No photograph or reproduction of any kind can convey the least idea of the veracity manifested in every detail of the Arnolfini picture. The original must be inspected with a magnifying-glass from point to point. It is only the likeness of a well-to-do merchant and his wife, standing in their own bed-chamber holding hands. The painter makes no attempt to flatter either them or their room. He might no doubt have found more traces of beauty in their faces had he cared to look for it; but he did not care, he looked for character, for the visible expression of the manner of folk they were—the husband quiet, dry, business-like, slow of speech and motion ; the wife simple, and rather childish in her simplicity, but dressed with matronly dignity; both of them orthodox, plain-dealing folk. Their room is like them. It is furnished with strong and taste-fully-made things—a fine bronze chandelier overhead, a handsome bedstead with an upright carved chair by the side, and a carved bench along the wall. Right opposite the spectator is a convex mirror set in a frame adorned with little medallion paintings of the Passion of Christ, as material for the lady's meditation whilst doing her hair. Her rosary hangs on a nail close by. The whole room is reflected

in miniature in the mirror, with the doorway at
which the spectator is supposed to be entering, and
a window in the passage without.   On the floor are
the clogs of John Arnolfini, neatly cut out of plain
wood, and behind are the more dapper foot-gear of
his wife.   There are many other little objects about,
such as an orange on the window-sill, placed there
to catch the light.   Through the window you can
see a cherry-tree, with sunshine on the ripe fruit.
In the treatment of these and similar details, Jan
van Eyck shows a liking for dots and spots of light.
He finds himself obliged to use a great deal of
shadow, but it is light that he loves and darkness
that he hates.   But light implies darkness, and cannot exist without it.   Nevertheless Jan does with as
little darkness as possible, and whenever he comes
across a space of general shadow he almost always
contrives to find there some fortunately-placed bright
object or another which reflects at all events a ray
of light.   Herein he shows himself akin to all the
later painters of the Dutch school, and indeed, almost
without exception, to the painters of all the northern
schools that came after him.   The Gothic painters
cared little for light and shade.   They put on their
colours in almost flat spaces, taking delight in the
graceful outlines of those spaces, but caring little about
the lights upon them or the shadows around them.
The beings they loved to depict lived in a land where

there was no night, and no burning heat, but where the Sun of Righteousness illuminated everything with his mild enveloping rays. The painters of the fifteenth century descended to earth and represented what they saw there as truthfully as they could, and so it came to pass that to depict the solid form of things was one of their first requirements, and to do that they must regard the lights and shades by which solid form is made manifest to the eye.

The excellence of the Arnolfini picture lies in the veracity with which the husband and wife are represented in pose, costume, and surroundings, and not merely in the truth of the portraiture of the faces. The character of the pair is manifested by their surroundings, and the spectator looks at these fully as much as, if not more than, he does at the faces.

The same is to a less degree the case with one of the gems of the Louvre Collection—Chancellor Rollin kneeling before the Madonna in a chamber overlooking the town of Maastricht. The Chancellor is to some extent known to us in history. He was a man of sumptuous life, who either out of generosity or pride founded monasteries, and was otherwise liberal to the Church. He seems to have been a learned man, and his great virtue was that he was "perfect in justice." In the Louvre picture, notwithstanding the splendour of colouring of the whole,

notwithstanding the amount and gorgeousness of the
jewelled ornaments on and about the Virgin, notwithstanding the loveliness of the garden, seen through
the window, and the perfection of the landscape with
its town and its river winding away to the far-off
range of snow mountains—it is not these things that
the eye chiefly regards. The face of the Chancellor,
hideous though it be, possesses a fascination, by
reason of its strong and vivid presentment of character,
which puts all else into the shade, and renders the
very Virgin and Child mere accessories in the
presence of the man who worships them. Jan has
taken the Chancellor at his ugliest, for he has painted
him with his brows knit into a frown and his lips
pressed together. He has reached that period of
life when the face loses all natural beauty and
depends for charm upon expression. If Rollin's
character was not pleasant, it was certainly strong.
He may well have been just, he may likewise have
been cruel. He looks like a man who regarded the
world with hostile severity. He has passed through
anxious times and emerged sour from the trial. His
expression, therefore, adds little that is attractive to
his features. Nevertheless, the downright veracity
of the painter's work, the clear insight and un-
trembling directness, which he shows, are worth a
hundred graceful saints and fluttering angels, the
incarnation of transient ideals, not human verities.

The altar-piece of the Madonna with Canon George
de Pala, now in the Academy at Bruges, presents, in
the portrait of the donor, the same fearless neglect
of all the artifices by which painters so often try
to flatter their subjects. The stout, somewhat asth-
matic old gentleman, grasping his prayer-book as
though for dear life, and kneeling with ponderous
emphasis at the foot of the Virgin's throne, is a piece
of pictured humanity that cannot be surpassed.
His heavy pudding-like character stares you in the
face, and you know the manner of man he is as soon
as your eye falls upon him. The artist might have
disguised all this, but Jan van Eyck would disguise
nothing. To tell the truth was his business, and he
told it without fear or favour. If he had been inclined to flatter anybody, it would surely have been
his wife in the picture he painted of her for present-
ation to the Painters' Guild of Bruges. He has, however, done nothing of the sort ; he has had her
dress in her best, with a fine fresh headdress such as
Arnolfini's wife wears, and he has set her down so,
the woman he knew, and whom we also may know.
The likeness is perfect. She is a bright, intelligent
housewife, with a clear, steady eye, and a firm mouth.
She has the look of a capable person. Her appearance is older than her years, for the inscription on
the frame of the picture states that she was thirty-
three at the time.

It must not, however, be imagined that Jan van Eyck is a mere realist in the ordinary sense. A realist is a man who looks at his subject, and sets down the superficial appearance of the thing, not selecting from what is visible with a definite purpose, but usually taking what is easy or effective, and leaving out what is difficult. Jan van Eyck selected with a definite purpose, namely, the expression of character. He took the man who was before him, and in painting his likeness he made every stroke tell something about the man's character. Thus his portraits are in the highest sense ideal; they are the visible expression of thought, not the reflections of sight.

The industry and veracity which were the secrets of his charm were likewise the secrets of his influence. They were to some extent communicable virtues. Thus the Van Eycks became the founders of a school in the widest sense. They did not merely influence their immediate pupils, but they influenced every artist who came in contact with their works. The Köln school became transformed after Jan van Eyck's day. Thenceforward, instead of Flanders being dependent upon the initiative of Köln in art, things were exactly reversed. The earnestness which produced such rich results in Jan was, at that time, a national characteristic; the artists of the day all possessed it more or less. Jan's work, therefore, quickly produced an effect. His initiative was swiftly responded to.

In the leading towns of Flanders and Brabant local schools arose, and the new technical method was employed, and the same ideals were adopted in all of them. Industrious, earnest work such as this, naturally led men along divergent ways, and local schools introduced modifications of one kind and another into the Van Eyck ideal ; but all these modifications were so slight, that until late years it was the custom in picture galleries to attribute any Flemish work to Van Eyck. A little careful study has enabled us to rectify such blunders, and to isolate from a multitude of school pictures, often of great beauty, the few real jewels which were the work of the leading men. The fact, however, that superficial students were able to mistake the works of so many different artists for that of the founder of the school, proves the strength of his influence over his contemporaries and followers.

The mystic school of Köln came to the end of its resources in two or three generations. The veracious school of Van Eyck lasted, we might almost say, for two centuries and a half. The seventeenth century painters of the Dutch and Flemish schools were the direct outcome of Van Eyck's initiative. Many of them contrived to employ his technique with little modification. Moreover, they

looked at things much in the fashion he had taught
them to look. It was their delight in the expression
of character that sent them to the peasantry for their
subjects, rather than to the high-born and the luxurious. It was their hatred of shams and their delight
in reality that made them prefer incidents in the life
of the fo'k to religious and other ideal subjects.
The initial direction that Jan van Eyck gave did
not require to be modified in any respect. The lines
he laid down were those ultimately followed; devi-
ations from them never led to a successful result in
the Low Countries. The mystic religious element
entered more strongly, as we shall see, into the work
of Roger van der Weyden and Hans Memling, than
into that of Jan van Eyck ; but so far from ennobling
their work, it prevented them from reaching the
altitude attained by their guide.

The only probably immediate pupil of Jan van
Eyck, whose works are known to survive, is Petrus
Cristus, or Christophorus. Two of his pictures are
preserved at Berlin, and the contrast between them
is of interest as confirming what has been said of
the master. The one is a pair of wings (signed and
dated 1452) from an altar-piece formerly at Burgos
in Spain. These contain representations of the
Annunciation, the Nativity, the Last Judgment, and
Hell. The first three are painted in a dull, perfunctory style. There is no trace in them of any

delight of the artist in his work; their design is
traditional; no artistic conception lies behind them.
The landscape below the Last Judgment, showing a
wide bay with surf breaking on the shore, stands on
a different footing; yet even there the artist does
but carry out the teaching he had received, without
improving upon it. It is only in the Hell that he
sets to work with vigorous hand and creative mind.
There, in the horrible gaping mouths, the rush of
fiery wind, the grim little fiends amongst the flames
inventing cunning tortures for the damned, and Death
spreading wide his wings of night over all, the painter
finds free play for such fancy as is in him, and fore-
tells the coming of Jerome Bosch. The other picture
(No. 532) is a small half-length portrait of an English
lady of the Talbot family. Here the artist has reality
before him, and he paints with all his heart. He
rounds the face with soft grey shadows all his own.
He makes indeed an error in the drawing of one
of the eyes, but none the less his picture presents
us with the reflection of a living person, whom we
can thus behold and know at the distance of four
centuries. His best picture is perhaps the 'Saint
Eligius' in the Oppenheim Collection at Köln. Were
it not for the halo one would certainly have taken this
for the earliest of that series of pictures of money-
changers which Quentin Massys and his fellows
painted with so much enjoyment. Saint or not,

however, it is all one to Petrus Cristus, so he have
an actual Fleming before him who can be represented in a room at Bruges busied with the ordinary
affairs of life. The very Annunciation, for Van Eyck,
took place in No. 26, Koey Straat, Ghent.

It is only passionately enthusiastic faith that can
enshrine itself nobly in work of religious art, and
passionate enthusiasm of faith was a thing impossible
to the Flemish mind in the fifteenth century. Religion became artificial in those days, and produced
many an unhealthy growth. Compared with the
work of Gothic artists the religious art of the Flemish
schools has slight fascination. The whole tone and
tendency of the day was opposed to soaring flights
of faith. Men were striving to penetrate facts, not
to invent fancies. They were being brought by the
irresistible force of events into contact with reality.
They were finding out that the most mysterious
of supernatural things are not the dreams of vision-
aries, but the actual men and women of the every-
day world. There was no diminution of reverence
implied in this. Reverence was being brought to
bear upon objects that for centuries had been held
in unjust scorn. The area of science and religion
were alike being enlarged. Contact with the actual
was producing not the annihilation but the elevation
of the ideal. The tendency of art to turn away
from visionary subjects and to busy itself about this

wondrous world came not a day too soon. The neglect with which the men of the thirteenth century treated themselves and their contemporaries had its noble side, but it deprived posterity of the power of being as strongly influenced and taught by them as it otherwise might have been. Artists work for the delight and instruction of posterity as well as of the people of their own day. The broader the base upon which art stands, the wider the range of purely human sympathies it enlists upon its side, the more powerful can it become, not only at a particular day, but as long as man remains the creature that he is. Buddhist art and Gothic art are admirable to those who force a way into the charmed area of the past. Greek art at its highest, Flemish portraiture, Elizabethan drama, are arts which address themselves to man as man, and cannot be forced by changing civilizations to lose their charm as long as the great feelings which all ages of men have felt alike retain their hold upon the human heart.

CHAPTER V.

THE generation of artists which succeeded the Van Eycks included several men of eminence. Owing, however, to the fact that they rarely signed their names to their pictures, and owing to the neglect with which the works of fifteenth-century art were treated by the men of the seventeenth and eighteenth centuries, many once famous painters have passed into total oblivion. No doubt some of their pictures still exist, but in many instances we know only the name and fame of a painter, but none of his works, whilst on the other hand we possess hundreds of pictures, but cannot say who they were by. The careful investigations of modern students in the history of art, and especially the patient labours of Mr. James Weale and M. Pinchart among the archives of Bruges and Brussels, have won back from oblivion the memory of certain well-nigh for-

gotten artists. Such was Roger van der Weyden.
The vague traditions connected with his name had
made it doubtful whether he was one man or four!
He was believed to be a pupil of Jan van Eyck's,
and pictures of the most diverse kinds of workmanship were indiscriminately attributed to him. It is
the fashion with certain superficial amateurs of art to
pour scorn upon the kind of study of ancient pictures
and records by which this state of ignorance has been
removed. Until ignorance on such fundamental
points as the authorship of a picture is replaced by
knowledge, the lover of art for its own sake has no
firm ground to go upon. He cannot begin to tell us
what he sees in the work of an individual until the
list of that individual's pictures is purged of all
productions falsely attributed to him.

Roger van der Weyden is the central figure
amongst the fifteenth-century artists of the Low
Countries. Jan van Eyck was both a greater man
and a greater artist than Roger, but Roger was the
greater master. The leading painters of the second
half of the century were either directly or indirectly
pupils of his. He was the agent who took the new
principles of Jan van Eyck and gave them currency,
not in the Netherlands alone, but throughout Germany
and even Italy. The fame of Jan van Eyck spread
abroad over Europe, and attracted to the Netherlands many young artists during the period of their

M

journeymanship, but then Jan (ob. 1440) was already dead, and so they naturally fell under the influence of his successor. The school of Köln in the days of the anonymous artist known to us as the "Master of the Lyversberg Passion" was nothing but an offshoot of Roger's school. Further up the Rhine at Colmar, Martin Schongauer, himself possibly an immediate pupil of Roger's, was influencing the whole course of German art. Even Wolgemut at Nürnberg, who was destined to become the master of Albrecht Dürer, did not escape the influence of the town-painter of Brussels.

It is as master rather than as artist that Roger's personality interests us. His pictures indeed are often of considerable beauty, but they by no means possess the artistic merit or the powerful individuality which belongs to the works of his great predecessor. Jan van Eyck's paintings are perennially delightful altogether apart from their historical position ; Roger's only yield their full value to a student who has acquired some knowledge of the effect which they produced upon the development of art. Van Eyck was great as a discoverer, Roger as an exponent. Van Eyck laid a broad and massive foundation, Roger carried out his predecessor's plans and devised the scaffolding by means of which the edifice was set up.

In order that Van Eyck's art should produce a

wide and general effect, a broadening of its ideal was to some extent necessary. Van Eyck's work is individual to the highest degree. It is the expression of a powerful personality, and cannot be confused with the product of any other mind whatever. Van Eyck forsook once and for ever the ancient religious ideal. In this he was acting in accordance with the tendency of his day, but he went ahead of the point to which that tendency had carried the ordinary level of his contemporaries. Roger van der Weyden, in the first place, reintroduced the religious element into Flemish art. He combined the old religious feeling with the new naturalism. He thus made it possible to enlist among his followers artists of various districts in which the old ideal retained hold of people's minds.

Roger was a native of the town of Tournai, where he was brought up and received his artistic education. He was already twenty-six years of age when he devoted himself to painting, and became the apprentice of Robert Campin. Unfortunately we know nothing about Robert Campin and the Tournai school of art in his days. Tournai is famous for its cathedral, the finest specimen of architecture on Flemish soil. It is stated to be a building which combines the elements of German, Romanesque, and French Gothic architecture. The painters of Tournai may be supposed to have come under a similar combination of influences. In all probability

M 2

the traditions of the old Köln school were stronger in them than in men working in the more advanced mercantile cities, whilst the Gothic-religious influence of France must have tended to keep alive in them the language of symbolism.*

The picture of the 'Seven Sacraments' in the Gallery at Antwerp is the best example we can produce of pure Tournai art. It is ascribed to Roger van der Weyden himself, though many critics fail to find the traces of his handiwork in it, and some would have us believe that it is by Robert Campin. At all events it is Tournai work, and was painted

* The three fine altar-pieces by Roger van der Weyden in the Berlin Museum show in a very plain and interesting fashion the decadence of the Gothic architectural spirit, which was going rapidly forward in his days, and the growth of the Renascence painting spirit in its place. The earliest of the three is certainly the John Baptist altar (534 B), of which the Städel Institute possesses a small copy. Here the three groups are surmounted by *pointed* stone-coloured arches, the fabric of arch and sculptures being the same colour. The spandrils are panelled. A true architectural feeling appears in the work. In the Miraflores Altar of the Joys and Sorrows of the Virgin (543 A), whilst the same general arrangement is adhered to, the arches are round and their heads are partly filled with lace-like tracery which could only have been carved in wood and has no structural function. The fabric and mouldings of the arches are painted brown, and only the sculptured groups and canopies are left their original stone-colour, so that they look as though glued on to the wall, and not carved out of it. In the Middelburg altar-piece (535) Roger takes a further step towards the Renascence, and omits all architectural accessories and canopies whatsoever.

between the years 1437 and 1460 for Jean Chevrot, bishop of that diocese.

It represents the interior of a church, obviously copied from some then existing building, not as yet identified. The nave of the church is depicted in the central panel, whilst the aisles with their side chapels are upon the wings. The foreground, in the midst of the nave, is occupied by a representation of the scene at Calvary, with the dead body of Christ upon the cross, the Virgin fainting in the arms of St. John and the three Maries weeping around. This is the historical event symbolized and commemorated by the various sacraments which derived their power from it. Thus immediately behind is a priest celebrating mass at the altar, and in the act of elevating the host. On the left side are the sacraments of Baptism, Confirmation, and Confession ; on the right those of Ordination, Marriage, and Extreme Unction. An angel holding a scroll hovers over each group engaged in the celebration of a sacrament. These angels are all of different colours, and their colours are symbolical. Thus the angel of baptism is white, the angel of marriage blue, the angel of ordination purple. Roger, as could be readily shown at some length, was fond of using colours in this symbolical fashion. Take for example his beautiful altar-piece, called of Miraflores,* now in the Berlin Museum. It

* Phot. Berlin Phot. Co.

represents three incidents in the life of the Virgin—
first her gladness over the new-born babe, secondly
her sorrow at the foot of the cross, and thirdly her
renewed and ever-enduring joy at the Resurrection.
In the first instance she is depicted as humble and
pure, so her robe is of white delicately tinted with
violet, and round the hem of it the embroidered
words, "My spirit hath rejoiced in God my Saviour,
for He hath regarded the lowliness of His handmaiden." In the second case she is shown in the
flood-tide of grief, and her robe is therefore blood-
red. Finally, in her renewed joy and completed
knowledge, she wears the blue of heaven, where all
is known and all is peace. Or again, likewise at
Berlin, is another very similar altar-piece,* representing three incidents in the life of John Baptist.
The central panel depicts the baptism of Christ. An
angel is waiting on the bank with the robe that the
newly baptized is thenceforward to wear. Its colour
is purple, the colour of the angel of ordination—
symbolic of passionate enthusiasm of self-sacrifice.

Roger's art then is essentially symbolic. An
emphatic instance of this is an altar-piece now at
Madrid† which there seems reason to believe was the
one painted by Roger for the Abbot of St. Aubert of
Cambrai. In this picture he evidently had in mind
the painting of the 'Seven Sacraments' already referred

* Phot. Berlin Phot. Co.   † Phot. Braun.

to. The central panel likewise presents a view into
the interior of a church, whilst in the foreground there
is again a Crucifixion. Painted and sculptured
incidents from the Passion are introduced into the
voussures of the archway admitting to the church.
The pilasters on either hand likewise bear painted
and sculptured groups illustrative of the remaining
six sacraments. On the right wing Adam and Eve
are driven out of the wooden gates of paradise
because of their sin, which is seen acted in the background. In the *voussures* and the spandrils are the
days of Creation. The left wing, on the contrary,
shows the Last Judgment, with the seven works of
mercy in the *voussures* and the spandrils. The
picture as a whole thus symbolized to the people of
Roger's day the Fall, the means of salvation, and the
final result upon those who accept or refuse those
means. The little groups of figures are a painted
commentary on the main subjects. The whole has
to be inspected closely, by a man in full religious
sympathy with the artist, before the lesson it conveys
can be learnt. The picture does not address itself to
the world upon the simple ground of a common humanity, as Jan van Eyck's pictures did, but it addresses
itself to people of a certain religion. . To appreciate
it you must give up all your own ideas, and you must
accept the painter's ideas. You must put yourself in
his place, and look at his work from his own point

of view, then you will find that it is excellent of its kind. This very quality which makes Roger's work less popular now than Jan van Eyck's made it more popular in Roger's day. Everybody was then a Christian of the old-fashioned Catholic type. Everybody understood and could appreciate work like this. The painter addressed the people of his day in the religious language of the day. Art being chiefly enlisted in the service of the Church, religious painting of this type produced a much more widespread effect, than the higher and more original work of a man who spoke to men merely as men, and that some century and a half before Shakespeare.

The two Berlin altar-pieces already referred to present the same characteristics as this altar of Cambrai. Each of the three main incidents is included under an archway embellished with sculptures which form a commentary upon it. Take for example the picture of Christ appearing to the Virgin after His resurrection. The Resurrection itself is seen occurring in the background just at the time when the three Maries are sorrowfully wending their way to the tomb, bearing their burden of ointments, and whilst the black clouds that have darkened the heavens are rolling away into the distance and melting into the blue of memory. The flowers are glad on every hand and the tender grass springs up in the bright morning sunshine. These are the preliminary incidents which serve to remind the spectator of the events which led up to the main event forming the subject of the panel. Overhead the sculptured groups tell the after-story of the Virgin's life—how the three Maries came and talked with her of the glad event, how she beheld her glorified Son ascend to heaven, how the Spirit came down upon her in Pentecostal fire, how an angel brought a palm-branch to her and foretold her passing away, how in the midst of the apostles she died and was carried up to heaven in glory and crowned by the Most High. Nor is this all; the sculptured capitals of the pillars bear images of Old Testament events—amongst them Samson carrying away the gates of Gaza, an accepted type of the Resurrection of Christ.

There is in the Picture Gallery at Munich an 'Annunciation'* which, by the introduction of such a sculptured commentary, betrays the influence of Roger. The apparition of the angel suggests to the painter the idea of miraculous apparitions in general, and sets him thinking on the subject. In order that he may transfer that train of thought to the spectator, he paints two sculptured medallions upon the wall of the room. One represents the apparition of the serpent to Eve, the other the apparition of the angel of God to Gideon ; the evil angel foreshadowing defeat, the good angel victory.

* Phot. Hanfstaengl.

We have thus far treated of the individual characteristics of Roger's as opposed to Van Eyck's art; of his religious and mystical tendencies as opposed to the whole-hearted naturalism of his great contemporary. But Roger could not escape the influence of Jan van Eyck, however much he might cling to his own ideals. It will be remembered that Van Eyck painted an altar-piece for Chancellor Rollin with a view of the city of Maastricht in the background. Roger was employed by the same munificent patron of the arts to paint a great altar-piece for the hospital at Beaune. He may thus have seen and been struck by the masterpiece of Van Eyck. At all events he, or some closely-allied follower of his, introduced an imitation of this landscape background into a picture of St. Luke drawing a portrait of the Virgin, which is now at Munich.* The picture was undoubtedly painted as altar-piece for a chapel of a painters' guild ; unfortunately, however, its history is not known. A comparison between these two landscapes in Van Eyck's and Roger's pictures shows what a great gulf lay between the two men in their love of Nature. Van Eyck's landscape is finished with marvellous accuracy, and manifests the artist's delight in every tiniest touch. Roger's, on the contrary, is perfunctorily treated, and resembles rather the work of an artist under the influence of Köln,

* Phot. Hanfstaengl.

where the painters preferred gold backgrounds to
distant natural features.

But the effect of Van Eyck upon Roger is visible
in more than the mere imitation of occasional details.
Not only did the method of painting invented by
the Van Eycks become the common medium of
artists throughout the Low Countries, but the spirit
of Jan's work infused itself into the art of the whole
school, even though it did not obliterate the old
religious tendencies all at once. Jan garnered in
the first crop of the new ideas which grew up in scattered quantities among his contemporaries. Those
ideas spread ever wider, and struck their roots more
deeply in the folk, till in the following century they
flourished everywhere. Thus, Roger could not be un-
influenced by them, and through the agency of Van
Eyck they infused themselves into his art.

The masterpiece of Roger van der Weyden contains in about equal measure the old religious ideal
and the new naturalism. This picture is the altar-
piece now at Berlin, painted for the church of
Middelburg,* at the command of the landlord of the
town, Bladelin, the treasurer of the Order of the
Golden Fleece. Bladelin, by the tenacity and uprightness of his character, raised himself from a
common burgher of the small town of Furnes to
be one of the leading men at the Court of the

* Phot. Berlin Phot. Company.

sumptuous Dukes of Burgundy. He was a Fleming
of the best type—a man of strong personality and
great fixity of purpose. For him, then, Roger painted
a picture, the subject being the first appearance of
Christ upon earth. The idea is embodied in three
simultaneously-occurring incidents. In the centre
is the new-born Babe adored by its parents, by
angels, and by Bladelin, an angel at the same time
announcing its birth to shepherds watching their
flocks on the distant hill. Upon the right wing the
Three Kings (repr.senting the Gentiles of the East)
behold the wonderful star in heaven with the child
in the midst of it, whilst upon the left wing the
Emperor Augustus (representing the Gentiles of the
West) sees the apparition of the Virgin and Child
in the heavens by the direction of the Tiburtine
Sibyl. Between this picture and Roger's earlier
works there are great and important differences. In
the first place there is no commentary here of
subsidiary incidents; the three incidents depicted
are all simultaneous, they are painted upon three
separate panels, and framed together as illustrative
of one idea, just as a modern painter might arrange
them. Secondly, the figures are of a portrait-like
character, if we except those of the Virgin and
angels. The Virgin still recalls the mystic Köln
type, though here it is more humanized than of old.
The slender hands and figure still symbolize ascetic

THE ADORATION OF THE MAGI. BY ROGER VAN DER WEYDEN. *Munich.*

purity, the brow tells of intellect passing the ordinary
gifts of men, the face of affection, the hair of fulness
of youthful life ; but in spite of all this the Virgin's
appearance is more that of an ordinary woman than
she ever possesses in a Köln picture of pre-Van
Eyck days. Humanity reigns supreme in all the
other figures. Bladelin is a splendid and veracious
portrait. The man stands visibly before us. So
again it is with the Emperor Augustus, who is really
Philip the Good. He lives ; he is a real man.
Roger had just returned from a prolonged visit to
Italy when he painted this picture ; perhaps while
there he had seen a portrait of Dante. At all events
one of the Emperor's courtiers bears some resemblance to the great Florentine. Between Jan van
Eyck's portraits and Roger's there is, however, a
whole world of difference. In Van Eyck's Madonna
with Chancellor Rollin, the Chancellor kneels phleg-
matically and undisturbed in the heavenly presence.
He might equally well be in his office. His face
is devoid of emotion, though it is full of character.
Roger, on the contrary, expresses character by means
of the emotion that a person betrays. The three
Magi do not pretend to adore ; their faces are full
of enthusiastic wonder. A still more striking example
may be drawn from the 'Adoration of the Magi' at
Munich,* a picture originally painted for the Church

* Phot. Hanfstaengl.

of St. Columba at Köln. The foremost of the three
Kings is Duke Philip the Good, the youngest of
them is his son Charles the Bold. The character
of Charles stands out plainly and unmistakably in
history. Bold he was even to rashness, alternately
generous and cruel, a man of hot passions, uncertain
in council, but vigorous to temerity in action. Just
such a man stands before us in the Munich picture,
but his character is expressed not in the settled
aspect of his face, as John would have made it, but
in the momentary glance of the eyes, puckering of
the brows, and pose of the figure. The stretched
uprightness of the form, the fierce holding of the
head, the thunderous aspect of the features, all work
together to convey to the spectator a notion of a
character altogether in keeping with that of the
Charles of History.

Thus Roger van der Weyden influenced his contemporaries and followers both as a portrait painter
and as a religious artist. He took the art of strong
character which Van Eyck originated and softened it,
infusing into it something of the religious tenderness
and mystery, and at the same time teaching his
fellow-artists to look at men not alone for the sake
of their monumental aspects, but with delight in the
momentary play of gesture and expression for which
the phlegmatic Jan had cared little.

As has been said, Roger's art, by reason of the

number of streams of style and tradition it united
in itself, was suited to produce a wide-spread effect.
South of the Alps his pictures were sought after and
his fame was known, all over certain his influence
was paramount, whilst in the Low Countries every
artist was his imitator if not directly his pupil. A
perfectly natural result followed. Roger's pictures
became types. In whatever fashion he represented a
subject other artists followed him. His pictures were
copied with more or less fidelity by numerous admirers, in a day when plagiarism in art was considered
an honest thing. Patrons would contract with a
painter for a picture to be like such and such a
work by a well-known artist. The most famous of the
types to which Roger gave currency was his design for
the Descent from the Cross. He repeated the subject
himself more than once, and his followers multiplied
his picture a hundredfold. It is not impossible that
the beautiful little triptych in the gallery of the Royal
Institution at Liverpool* may represent the first
stage of the idea in the painter's mind. The picture
itself may not be by Roger, but our knowledge of the
details of his life is so small, and our acquaintance
with the growth of his style and his early methods of
work is so vague, that we cannot pronounce definitely
about a good many works which strongly suggest his

* See photograph in W. M. Conway—Gallery of Art of the
Royal Institution, Liverpool.

N

authorship. This is one of such, and belongs to a group of pictures all painted in the same style, in Roger's studio and under his eye, and very likely by his hand. The figures in the Liverpool triptych correspond in sentiment and character with those in the great altar-piece, painted by the master in the period of his fully-developed powers, and now hanging in the gallery at Madrid.* They are not individually so graceful nor individually so expressive ; but they give evidence of the artist's struggle to express more than he yet had power to do. The wings of the Liverpool picture bear pictures of the two thieves on their crosses. At Frankfort is a panel painted with a life-size replica of the thief who appears on the right wing. The bottom of the panel has been sawn off, and so only the heads of Longinus and the Centurion appear on it. This panel points to the existence of two wings like the Liverpool wings, only larger. These two wings may have belonged to the Madrid picture, the wings of which are gone. If so, Roger, when he painted the Madrid picture, had this earlier work in his mind ; he modified and greatly improved the composition of the central panel ; but he kept the old designs of the wings in the main unaltered, and gave them to a good pupil to carry out. It is at all events certain that the wings of the final picture did contain thieves of this type, for we

* Phot. Braun and Laurent.

CHRIST TAKEN DOWN FROM THE CROSS. BY ROGER VAN DER WEYDEN. *Madrid.*

N 2

fortunately possess an engraving,* done by an early Flemish master, and rudely copied from Roger's great picture (or from a copy of it), and in this engraving the two thieves appear, copied in reverse as they naturally would be. There exist many more copies, and perhaps one replica by the master himself. The type soon became recognized, and for more than half a century artists seldom diverged far from it in painting this subject. The existence of the engraving just referred to, has led to a suggestion that possibly Roger engraved it himself. As an art for the production of prints for sale, engraving upon a copperplate arose during his life-time, and it was first chiefly practised in the district of the Lower Rhine. It is *primâ facie* probable that the earliest engravers were gold-smiths. It is likewise probable that the art was known and practised in the studio of Roger. The earliest engravers were imbued with Roger's principles of design, and the first great engraver, the so-called 'Master E. S.,' was powerfully influenced by our master. In the year 1449 Roger went to Italy, and it has been suggested that he made Italian artists acquainted with the new method.

Unfortunately we know little about the details of Roger's life. The main incident in it was his appointment to be town-painter of Brussels, in which

* The only known impression is at Hamburg; M. Hymans published it.

city he dwelt during the active years of his life, and there he died and was buried in 1464.

Even more tantalizing is another great artist who, already probably a man of middle age, became a master-painter in the Ghent Guild about the time of Roger's death. During his Netherlands journey Dürer was taken into St. Jacob's church at Bruges, and shown "the precious pictures by Roger and Hugo." "They were both great masters," he says. About a certain portion of Hugo's life we are tolerably well informed. He lived for a decade or so in Ghent, with his hands full of work. His chief employment seems to have been the painting in lime-colours of great linen sheets to take the place of tapestry. Records and accounts remain to tell us how, on certain festive occasions, the walls of houses were hung with the workmanship of Hugo. He painted quickly and upon a large scale in this manner, and his storied sheets became popular. In Bruges and Ghent many churches and houses owed their mural hangings to the deft brush of Master Hugo. Of all this, however, not one atom remains. But Hugo was no stranger to oil-painting. The picture Dürer saw and praised was doubtless such, and at any rate Van Mander, the historian of Flemish art, knew several of Hugo's pictures and valued them highly. All these however, if they anywhere exist, have gone into forgetfulness, with one single exception—

the altar-piece in the Hospital of Santa Maria Nuova
in Florence. Towards the end of his life he seems to
have suffered from religious melancholy, and so he
retreated to the Augustinian Convent of Roodendale.
A fellow-monk has left us an account of the painter
which is of such interest that no apology is required
for introducing it here. He says: " I was a novice
when Van der Goes entered the convent. He was so
famous as a painter that men said his like was not to
be found this side the Alps. In his worldly days
he did not belong to the upper classes ; nevertheless,
after his reception into the Convent, and during his
novitiate, the Prior permitted him many relaxations
more suggestive of worldly pleasure than of penance
and humiliation, and thus awakened jealousy in
many of our brothers. Frequently noble lords, and
amongst others the Archduke Maximilian, came to
visit him and admire his pictures. At their request
he received permission to remain and dine with them
in the guest-chamber. He was often cast down by
attacks of melancholy, especially when he thought of
the number of works which he still had to finish ; his
love of wine, however, was his greatest enemy, and for
that at the strangers' table there was no restraint.
In the fifth or sixth year after he had taken the
habit, he undertook a journey to Köln with his
brother Nicolas and others. On his return journey
he had such an attack of melancholy that he would

have laid violent hands on himself had he not been forcibly restrained by his friends. They brought him under restraint to Brussels, and so back to the Convent. The Prior was called in, and he sought by the sounds of music to lessen Hugo's passion. For a long time all was useless; he suffered under the dread that he was a son of damnation. At length his condition improved. Thenceforward of his own will he gave up the habit of visiting the guest-chamber and took his meals with the lay-brothers." In the year 1482 he died.

Our only certain relic of this remarkable man's work is the picture at Florence, above referred to. It was painted at the order of Tommaso Portinari, the agent at Bruges for the banking-house of the Medici at Florence. Of all foreigners resident in Bruges this Tommaso was the most splendid and influential. He was man of affairs and political ambassador as much as merchant. Though so far away from his Florentine home he was not forgetful of her, and amongst other acts of munificence the donation of a great altar-piece to the Hospital of Santa Maria Nuova was by no means the most generous. This was the picture which Hugo painted.

Of all fifteenth-century Flemish works remaining to us this picture is the largest. Hugo was so much accustomed to painting on a large scale, that the little gems his contemporaries loved to work at pro-

bably possessed small fascination for him. The
monk's account suggests him to us as a man of energy
and dash, suffering often from nervous reactions, but
when at work loving to work with vigour. Perhaps
the largeness of his treatment was more acceptable to
the fresco-loving Italians than the fine finish of other
northern artists. The Florentine picture at all events
affords a strong contrast when compared with other
contemporary works. Northern painters, when they
had a large picture to make, usually broke it up into
numerous small panels containing each a separate
subject, treated as a separate picture. Hugo, when
large work was ordered of him, rejoiced to be able to
handle it upon a large scale. He painted the figures
the size of life, and introduced relatively few of them.
He made no attempt to pack the area at his disposal;
on the contrary, his composition errs by being somewhat too loose and open.

The central panel of the altar-piece represents the
Nativity. The Virgin kneels before the new-born
babe ; Joseph, having kicked off his sandals, adores
from a remoter point ; angels with splendidly-coloured
wings and robes, kneel around or hover in the air,
some arising like gathering birds, not without a
certain grostequesness of effect. From one side the
shepherds with their crooks are just arriving to
behold the new-come wonder. The left wing of the
picture is occupied by the kneeling donor, Portinari,

with his two boys, St. Anthony and St. Thomas, standing behind. His wife and daughters, with their patron saints, Magdalen and Margaret, occupy the other wing. A glance is enough to show that Hugo was not much influenced by Roger van der Weyden. The lesser angels in the air somewhat recall his creations, but in the rest of the picture there is little to remind us of him. Hugo clearly was more directly the offspring of Jan van Eyck, and this will become evident as we proceed. In character he was not by nature religious or mystical. He loved good cheer; he was of a passionate disposition. One story preserved about him relates how he fell violently in love, and painted a picture of himself and his lady, under the guise of David and Abigail—of course, however, the picture is lost. He took to a religious life through fear of hell, a common form of mania; but he was in no sense a man of religious tendency. On the contrary, even Jan van Eyck was not so great a naturalist as he. Every one of the faces in Hugo's picture is a portrait, and a portrait of extraordinary power. Portinari appears as a man of dignified bearing; his boys behind him, though for a moment quelled into quietness, are boys every inch of them, full of the potentiality of mischief and fun. Equally good and characteristic are the lady and her little girl, whilst of the female Saints behind, St. Mary Magdalen is the finest full-length figure of a woman ever produced in

THE NATIVITY. BY HUGO VAN DER GOES. *S. Maria Nuova, Florence.*

Flanders in those days. Her thoughtful and characteristic face, her dignified pose, and her splendid garments, are all interesting to a reflective spectator. Nevertheless, it is evident that the painter's interest was greater in other parts of the picture. It is the heads of the rough old men and peasants that he painted with the greatest delight. The picture of Portinari shows that he could depict a perfect gentleman when he pleased, but when he had to draw the figure of a male saint, instead of taking his model from among the high-born and refined (as the Italians always did), he went to peasants for inspiration. It is clear that he himself was a man of the folk. Art in his days was beginning to draw its life from a wider area, and to address a wider public than before. The spread of the rapidly-developing method of wood-carving was bringing artists and the folk together, and artists were receiving new strength from the contact. This picture of Master Hugo's would be of untold value for one thing alone, even if it possessed no other virtues: it is the first picture that really makes us acquainted with the mediæval peasantry. Nothing is more obvious than that the three shepherds are drawn from life. They are no ideal shepherds; their horny hands, rough features, and gaping mouths, are proofs of a perfect veracity. The next artist whose mind was in sympathy with the peasant class was Dürer, and a comparison between these shepherds and the country-folk engraved by him is rich in suggestiveness. Most of the writers of that period either scorn the labouring agricultural folk as people without soul, or wholly omit to mention them. Not many years later the miserable course of events was about to give rise to the Peasants' War with all its train of horrors. ¡Then the folk were abused by high and low, reviled, hated, trodden down, and cursed, From the accounts preserved to us from those days of rage we derive most of our misinformation about the country-folk of mediæval times. Dürer's prints and Hugo's picture tell a wholly different and an obviously more truthful tale. The three men in this Nativity, or at all events two of them, are not creations issuing from the moral consciousness of any one. They are reflections of actual persons. Their bent figures tell of their labouring battle with the earth. Their hardened faces have been beaten into that rugged form by nights of exposure, frost, and storm. Whilst the world was going along in its noisy fashion with wars and revolutions, setting up of kings, political intrigues, and tremblings of hope and fear in the hearts of conspicuous but now for the most part forgotten men, peasants such as these were the real heat that kept the whole surface bubbling on the go. But for their careless and continuous labour, kings and feudal systems would have faded in a few days. Yet they

are as unrecorded and unobserved (except for some
tyrannous statute of labourers or another) as if the
fine gentry, the monks and the merchants, had really
been the life at the heart of the whole body politic.
Among the multitude of Golden-Fleeced Heroes,
Hanseatic merchants, Lords, Counts, Dukes, and
Popes, whose likenesses we possess, whose sayings
we can know if we care to hunt them up, whose
manner of living is recorded in minute detail, these
three old shepherds are the only representatives of
the far larger and more important body of silent
sufferers and silent workers who kept the world
a-going. And mark what manner of men they are!
Not soulless ruffians by any means, not cattle nor
anywhere on the level of cattle, but strongly intelligent
creatures, capable of wide-mouthed wonder, of reverent
delight—human to the uttermost, warm of heart and
keen of eye, though coarse in manner and slow of
utterance.

In such veracity and strength of handling Hugo
shows himself a true follower of Van Eyck. He
surpasses him in the expression of reverence, and he
nearly equals him in the expression of character,
though he falls far behind him in the artistic quality
of his work. Every picture of Jan's has an aspect of
inevitableness. It seems as though everything must
have been just so. There is nothing to alter, nothing
to improve. The harmony of colouring, the balance

of masses, the arrangement of accessories, is always as good as can be ; and Jan's handling of the brush as a vehicle for laying on paint has never been surpassed. Hugo was less richly endowed with these artistic qualities. In Van Eyck they were partly the gift of nature, but more the reward of patience. Hugo was not a patient man. He was of a hot and hurried disposition. Thus his work is less well planned than his predecessor's. The grouping of his figures is faulty ; they are patched together rather than grouped. The accessories all about are often in the way. The design of such a picture as this Nativity required more consideration than it received. A figure wanted taking out here, another introducing there. The whole thing is to pieces, and the eye fails to receive much pleasure from it as a whole.

One more point must be noticed before we close this altar-piece—it is the treatment of light. We have already noticed Jan van Eyck's love of brightness ; here the feeling is more strongly manifested still. It is usually said that in this picture the light proceeds from the Child ; it does not, however, do anything of the sort, as a glance at the shadow cast by the Virgin's figure conclusively shows. The light falls from above upon the Child, in a mysterious manner, and then is reflected upwards from the floor. Thus the whole picture is solidified by reflected lights in a bold and original way. The reflections upon the two angels, close above in the air, are particularly carefully done, and no other picture of this date, except a little panel in the Belvedere at Vienna, shows anything of the kind. As compared with Jan van Eyck's treatment, the shadows are darker here. Hugo, to give emphasis to his light, increases the surrounding darkness. In fact he takes another step along the road that was to lead to Rembrandt. The germ of that lurid gloom, which the fiery Dutchman was one day to light up with his mysterious cunning, lies before us here. The same spirit belongs to both artists. Some painters rejoice in colour; they are usually happy men, full of gaiety and simpleness of heart. Others look first for light, if it be but a far-off glimmer, to pierce the gloom that shrouds them in. They are for ever praying the prayer of Ajax; they are men upon whom the stress of things lies heavy. They wait for light, but behold obscurity; for brightness, but they walk in darkness. The art of all such men is an intellectual art. They paint to satisfy the thoughts rather than to delight the eye. This is no empirical generalization, it is a demonstrable truth. Take the great chiaroscurits of bygone schools—Rembrandt, Tintoret, Lionardo da Vinci, Jan van Eyck, Turner,—every one of them is a man of deep thought, on the whole, sad. Take the colourists in their turn—Bellini, Cima, Giorgione,

O

Titian, Holbein, Reynolds; as far as we know, or
can infer anything about them, they were without exception joyous. Follow out the comparison amongst
the poets, and you will find the same result; those
who are always telling of the colours of things are
happy; those who speak of the light upon things
are thoughtful, and usually terribly in earnest.
When

> " The white lime glimmered, and the trees
> Lay'd their dark arms about the field ;
> A hunger seized my heart,"

says Tennyson. Hungry of heart, likewise, was
Hugo, if his picture tells the truth, and what else
can it tell? Such also the brief story of his life as
we know it reveals him. The light of history touches
him but slightly, though with brightness where it
does touch him, leaving a vacant midnight all around.
Nevertheless, the few lineaments thus brought into
prominence are enough to reveal an artist nature of
peculiar interest—a man of power, originality, and
restless heart, alternately carried to the heights, and
plunged into the depths. Fond of his fellow-men and
joyous with them, lightly undertaking a load of work
in a sanguine hour, then miserable when the weight
of it rests upon him and the enthusiasm has faded
for awhile away. A man of strong though perhaps
hardly lasting. affections, a man of clear observation,
of considerable insight into character, of wide sym-

pathy for the outcast and the poor. Finally, a man of truth, veracious in the utterance of his handicraft, and earnest, like her of Cumæ, that his last words be true. Of all the treasures of which we have been robbed by Time and the rage of men one against another, assuredly the memorials of so rich a mind are not amongst the least precious.

CHAPTER VI.

THE law of attraction holds good in the artistic as in the material world. No school of art can attain strength without influencing neighbouring schools. Such influence is sometimes a power for good. The school of Siena was strengthened by contact with the genius of Giotto, and the school of Florence was refined by contact with the works of Simone Martini. As often as not, however, such influence produces evil effects. When the artists of the Low Countries formed the habit of studying in Italy, the level of their work was depressed, and the same result followed in Köln when the works of Flemish painters began to be imitated there.

The school of Köln, as has been sufficiently stated, took form under the moulding force of a restricted but refined ideal. It was not the ideal of a great civilization, but of a relatively small clique of men. It would not, therefore, spread far or last long without

R.B.X.A.

ST. GEREON AND THE THEBAN LEGION.

To face p. 196.

losing its strength and purity. Thus, early in the fifteenth century, it began to wear out. It had by that time attained sufficient expression, and the buyers of pictures became tired of it. Just then Art was advancing with rapid strides in Flanders under the leadership of the Van Eycks. Köln stood in close relation with the Low Countries, and no conspicuous movement could stir them without being felt in the Rhenish City. Köln artists did not attempt to stem the tide ; headed by Meister Stephan, they drifted willingly with it.

We know little about this Meister Stephan, and his very name has only been preserved to us by an entry in Dürer's diary of his Netherlands journey. Archives prove that Stephan Lochner bought a house in Köln in 1442, and that he died in 1451. His great work, painted at some time during the second quarter of the fifteenth century, was the altar-piece for the Chapel of the town-hall, now the most valuable painting in Köln Cathedral.* It is to be considered as the typical example of the second period of the Köln school. Compared with earlier large altars, it presents this difference, that, instead of representing a multitude of incidents on different panels, it represents one incident on all three. The Virgin, friendly yet majestic, sits in the midst with the child on her lap. The Three Kings,

* This and all the principal pictures at Köln are photographed by Crefeld, formerly Raps, of Köln.

patrons of Köln, kneel around, and their followers
stand behind them. On the wings are the faithful
companies of Köln's martyrs—Ursula and her maidens,
Gereon and his fellows of the Theban Legion. The
ground is carpeted with fairest flowers, increasing in
number and richness as they approach the Virgin's
feet. The background is of diapered gold, with the star
of Bethlehem upon it, shining forth from a company
of little cherubs, who hover in glad reverence around.
A florid arcading, as of carved wood, runs all across
the top of the panels, reminiscent of the time when
painted figures formed cheap substitutes for statues
in Gothic niches.

The modernising element is supreme throughout the
whole picture. The Virgin and Saints are clothed,
not in the ideal drapery of an imagined Paradise, but
in the costly costumes of a fifteenth-century court.
The knightly saints wear the armour of the day, part
plate, part chain. All the faces, except perhaps those
of the Virgin and St. Ursula, are portrait-like and
animated. In these respects, as well as in the type of
the female faces, Flemish influence is clearly visible.
The strong and masterful art of the practical Flemings
is bending the pliant product of Köln.

There is little or no decay visible in Meister
Stephan's pictures, but they contain those foreign
principles from which decay was to arise. There is
more freedom of pose and more naturalism. The

The Marriage of the Virgin. By the Master of the Lyversberg Passion. *Munich.*

•

figures are not the mere expression of mild and tender characters. They are individuals with the weaknesses as well as the virtues of humanity. The old beauty of outline is now sacrificed to truth of form in limb and drapery. Characters and expressions are more manifold. More figures are introduced, and they are united together without relation to any sculpturesque unity in the grouping, and without thought as to the elegance of outline of the whole when projected against a gold background. Their grouping is governed by pictorial and sentimental necessity alone. Most of these changes were not in themselves harmful; but an art of this new character was not suited to express the old Köln ideal of an idyllic world, and artists trained by that ideal would not adopt with a whole heart the new ideal of an all-round humanity which their practically-minded contemporaries had developed in the Low Countries.

But Köln art did not suddenly go out. It had many decades of activity still before it, during which work worthy of praise was produced by more than one now anonymous artist. There was, for instance, the 'Master of the Heisterbach altar,' a picture whose various panels are now at Köln, Munich, and Schleissheim. He was a follower of Stephan's, who also harked back to Meister Wilhelm, and learnt anew from his work something of the old grace of manner and mildness of expression. Perhaps it was he who painted a large picture of St. Ursula sheltering her maidens under her cloak, which we may see in the Köln Museum (No. 124). a painting not without elements of grandeur as well as grace.

Then there is a many-panelled altar, once in the Lorenz Church at Köln, and now scattered in the Museums of Köln, Frankfort, and Munich. Its central panel (at Köln) bears a famous representation of the Last Judgment. Here all the weird fancies of the Teutonic heart find utterance as clearly as they did in Petrus Cristus' picture already described. There is a realism in the expression of faces and figures amongst the damned almost passing to the verge of caricature.

The most charming of the Köln painters of the last half of the fifteenth century was the 'Master of the Lyversberg Passion.' He was not, however, uniformly sweet as his predecessors had been; it was only in subjects of family life, such as the ' Birth of the Virgin,' to which reference was made above, that he preserved the distinctive qualities of the mystic school. Turn from that to the series of Passion-pictures from which the artist takes his name, and a wholly different personality seems to speak from the panels. The Passion, as conceived by this painter, was a scene for the display of brutality, rather than the exhibition of heroism. The enduring Christ is not the subject of the pictures, but the torturing villains that surround him. The figure of Christ does not dominate the rest ; the vile element seems always victorious. Such interest as the pictures possess lies in the delineation of ruined characters. The faces of the Jews are terribie for plain expression of vileness. Christ is a mere weary creature, enduring because He must, and not even conscious of a high ideal. The only touch of sweetness is the tender, though rather unreal, sorrow of the Maries. Moreover, after pondering over this picture well, it becomes apparent that the vileness and coarseness in them are not those of a wild, undeveloped art, but of an art corrupted and decaying. The singleness of aim is gone from the school. Artists have learnt to admire something foreign to the ideal by which they had been formed ; they mistook brutality for strength ; they tried to combine the new ideal with their old traditions. As a body they failed, and their failure is instructive.

We need not further follow the fortunes of the school of Köln. Such masters as those named after the St. Thomas' altar, or the picture of the ' Death of the Virgin,' are little interesting for their own sake. They have to be considered in connection with the growth of the later German schools, but they may be omitted in the present connection. The chief personal influence experienced by the Masters of the Lyversberg Passion and the St. Thomas' altar was that of Roger van der Weyden, or perhaps even of his pupil, Dierick Bouts of Louvain. Roger van der Weyden's influence was one which it was almost impossible for any artist of the last half of the fifteenth century to escape. His power was felt from Ferrara to Burgos, and from Portugal to Paris. The reasons for this permeation of it must be sought in its nature and the conditions of the time.

Roger, as has been shown, borrowed Jan van Eyck's technical methods, but mingled in with Jan's ideal of broad humanity some of the old religious qualities. Roger's art is thus not so universal for all time as Jan's, for whilst Jan's was founded on the broad basis of humanity, Roger's ideal depended upon the taste and creed of a day. But for this very reason Roger's art was better suited to spread. The Church was still, directly or indirectly, the chief patron of art. Her ideals still ostensibly reigned supreme. An art which was to cover Europe must at any rate have a religious appearance. Jan's style was too original, too personal to the man himself, to go very far without some intermediary to popularize it. Jan's name was the great attraction which brought students to the Low Countries ; but, arrived there, it was in Roger's school that they worked, and it was Roger's impress that they took away with them.

Streams of style, like all other civilizing influences, follow the course of trade. Consider for a moment the growth of the printer's craft, and this fact becomes at once apparent. The chief internal trade-routes of Europe were the water-ways. Towns within one river-system were likely to be more closely united than towns on different river-systems. If now we divide central Europe into its river-basons, we shall find that each river-bason in the main has its school of printing. There is a family likeness between the works of Rhine printers, and a different family likeness between the works of printers in the Maas valley. This is one of the keen generalizations which the wide and minute learning of the greatest of bibliographers, the late Henry Bradshaw, availed to demonstrate. In like manner it was because the artists of Flanders worked in the market-place of the world's commerce that they were enabled to carry their influence so far. Flanders was at one end of the chief trans-European trade-route. Flemish ships sailed to all European ports. Whatever therefore the Low Country artists accomplished that was worthy of imitation soon found imitators in many lands.

Brussels was the head-quarters of Roger's activity. The most active part of his career was from about 1451, when he returned from Italy, till his death in 1464. During those years he brought Flemish influence to bear upon most of the art-schools of Europe. At home the painters dominated all other artists. The weavers of tapestry, the sculptors in wood and stone, the glass-painters, the metal-founders, the engravers of monumental brasses—all followed the fashions set by the painters. These different groups of craftsmen were then at the head of their several crafts in all Europe. Dürer relates how his father, the goldsmith, spent "a long time with the great artists in the Netherlands" before he settled in Nürnberg. As with the goldsmiths so was it also with most of the artistic crafts of Europe. Young workmen flocked from all parts in their years of journeymanship to learn style from the greatest living masters in the Low Countries. Roger's influence upon the craftsmen of his own country thus received wide extension. In a brief sketch it is impossible to do more than trace some of its bolder effects, and in order to accomplish this with the less uncertainty, it will be well to select a few particular examples, leaving them to fulfil a representative function. Four artists then shall be considered in turn : the engraver called the 'Master E. S. of 1466,' the engraver and painter Martin Schongauer of Colmar, the engraver and painter Michel Wolgemut of Nürnberg, and the painter Hans Holbein the Elder of Augsburg.

The Master 'E. S.' was the first great engraver of Northern Europe Martin Schongauer, almost a contemporary of his, was the second great engraver, and carried the art to a higher point of development than any other artist till the coming of Dürer. Engraving, so far as the North is concerned, first attained the rank of an art in the neighbourhood of Roger. One of the earliest existing prints is from an engraving after Roger's 'Descent from the Cross.' Engraving was not of course invented by Roger or any pupil of his. There were probably many centres from which the art took its rise. Any time for centuries the method of printing engravings might have been put into practice, had there been any popular demand for cheap works of art. Artists had long been accustomed to engrave monumental brasses and details of goldsmith's work. Probably the taking of impressions from small engraved plates, such as goldsmiths frequently made for ornamental purposes, was a process well known to workmen as one of the ordinary methods for testing the progress of their work. Printing in one form or another is a much older process than people think, even leaving the Chinese out of the question. Patterns were printed on pieces of stuff all through the Middle Ages. It has been recently stated that there is, amongst Archduke Rainer's *papyri*, a piece of paper on which Arabic prayers were printed in the ninth century. What determined the application of engraving to the purpose of multiplying prints was not any fortunate discovery made by some lucky individual, but the growth of a popular need which could only thus receive satisfaction. The popular demand for cheap works of art arose in the more advanced parts of Europe about the middle of the fifteenth century, and engraving and printing quickly flourished everywhere in response to it. The important question is not who first printed from an engraved plate, but what man or set of men first made it a definite part of their life's work to engrave plates for the sake of the multiplication and sale of impressions from them. It seems probable that this was done in the lower part of the Rhine valley at the time when the arts of that district were ruled by Roger van der Weyden. At all events, the first engravers of the North worthy the name of artists were pupils or imitators of Roger, and the most notable amongst them was 'E. S. of 1466.'

He is called of 1466 from a date found on several of his best prints, but others are forthcoming with the years 1461, 1464, and 1467 signed upon them. We do not know his name, nor the place of his birth, nor anything for certain about him except what we can gather from his works themselves. Their spirit suggests that he was a native of the Rhine valley. The mystic ideal is stronger in him than in Roger. His style of design, however, bears Roger's impress. The scenes of his activity were various. He is found at one time working for the Burgundian court, at others appearing in different German towns. He must have visited the pilgrimage resort of Einsiedlen, for he engraved two plates of the famous Madonna of that place. His works are numerous, and he had many followers. There are altogether two hundred different existing prints by him or his assistants.

His most famous engraving is the larger of the two Madonnas of Einsiedlen. It is signed E., and dated 1466. In this work the German element predominates over the Flemish, but the influence of Flanders is there. The general arrangement of subject is as follows. A gallery at the top supports a group consisting of the Trinity surrounded by a choir of angels. This gallery symbolizes Heaven. Under it is the shrine of Einsiedlen, where the Virgin sits above the altar with the Child upon her lap, a holy abbot standing on one side of her and an angel on the other. Pilgrims reverently stand or kneel upon the chapel floor. The origin of this arrangement is not Flemish ; it is wholly and particularly German. In fact, it is borrowed from the mystery plays, so common all over Europe and especially in Germany in the fifteenth century. The Mysteries were originally acted in Church, and then the rood-loft was used to represent heaven, a stage erected below it symbolized the earth, whilst the floor of the nave was the place of the devils and the damned. The actors of Mysteries, driven from the church into the market-place, as by the fifteenth century they almost every-

P

where had been, still employed a similar arrangement for their stage. Thus the gallery of heaven in the engraving is directly borrowed from the stage arrangements of the Mysteries. The architecture of the chapel is the debased German Gothic of the day, and possesses no peculiarly Flemish elements. It is in the technique and the figures that Flemish influence must be sought.

When considering the figures three factors have to be taken into consideration : the old traditions and influences of the mystic school of Köln, still alive in such artists as the Westphalian painters, and the Master of the Lyversberg Passion ; the traditions and influences of the old schools of wood-sculpture in all parts of Germany and the Low Countries ; the new realistic tendency which was more clearly manifested in the Low Countries than elsewhere, but which was not peculiar to them, being the inevitable tendency of art all over Europe. The presence of these three factors is visible in this engraving.

The whole conception of the design descends from the mystics. The company of angels around the Trinity, the actual presence of the Virgin in her shrine, the devout expressions of the pilgrims, all come from this source. Had the Köln school never existed this print would have been otherwise designed.

The influence of the schools of wood-sculpture is

even more visible. The normal old German altar-
piece was not a picture but a great pile of carving
flanked by two doors, which shut up over it like a
box. These doors, or wings, as we call them, were
primarily intended to keep the carvings clean. They
had to be decorated, and so their panels were more or
less roughly painted. By degrees the painting of the
panels improved until we find such wings as those
upon which the Lyversberg Passion was painted;
but the painted wings were always subordinate to the
carved wood centre-piece. The wood-carver did not
trust to his chisels alone for his effect. His work
was not complete till the whole of it had passed
under the hands of the painter and emerged gay with
colour and bright with gold. The Einsiedlen print
has a conspicuous aspect of solidity. The background of the chapel is dark, and the figures are
strongly relieved against it. Moreover, the whole
depth of the picture could easily have been rendered
in sculptured wood. There are in it no large open
spaces or wide-extending vistas, difficult of translation
into sculpture and bas-relief.

Consider further how the nature of the material
employed by the wood sculptor must have influenced
and visibly did influence the character of his sculptured figures. Toughness and grain are the two
important qualities of wood. It yields easily to a
sharp tool, yet its toughness makes the carving

durable. Moreover, it is possible to cut wood deeply
and into thin pieces. A much sharper relief can be
carved in wood than in stone. Wood can be under-
cut more deeply. Small thin pieces can be left
standing out separate from the mass. All this is
rendered possible by the toughness of the material.
On the other hand, the grain is a master which must
be obeyed. It is easier to cut along it than across it.
Ridges and filaments of wood are only strong if they
run with the grain. Straight forms are more readily
produced in one direction and curved forms in others.
Thus the nature of the wood enters as a factor into
the design ; the designer must bear the grain in mind
or his design will have to be modified in execution.
The human figure carved in wood naturally tends to
present certain characteristics. Subtly curved surfaces
being difficult to render, the nude is no oftener introduced than can be helped. Sculptured wooden figures
are generally draped. The surface does not admit of
fine working up like the surface of marble ; forms are
therefore boldly rather than delicately rendered, and
paint and gilding are acceptable aids. Drapery
consists of large, almost flat spaces broken by angular
bends and folds.

All these characteristics of design mark the figures
of the Einsiedlen print. The choir of angels could
be carved in wood without modification ; the robes
which hang over the parapet are more suited for

carving than painting. A school of artists nurtured in the use of paint would not have designed
such drapery. The same is even more the case with
the figures under the archway. The drapery outlines
are all long and straight; the figures are buried
inside their garments. The nude figure of the child
Christ is the feeblest part of the whole. All the
faces, moreover, are boldly rendered. Few of them
have much charm of feature; their parts are sometimes wrongly and always roughly proportioned.
The hair of the bearded men is specially reminiscent
of wood-sculpture. The peculiar dragging back of
the beard against the chest was a natural expedient
for strengthening the neck of a wooden figure.

On to this old German stock the 'Master E. S.'
grafted the vivifying influence of Flanders. Van
Eyck had raised the northern schools to the level
of expressive art; before him painters had been
content to convey a religious idea. Jan van Eyck
made his pictures primarily expressive of pictorial
ideas. They were fine works of art, apart from all
question of meaning; finely executed and finished
things. Therefore the meaning with which they were
weighted smites the spectator with previously unex-
ampled force. Again, Jan painted individuals, not
personified qualities. He gave each figure an all-
round and not a one-sided character. Roger, as has
been said, mingled something of this individualism

with the old religious spirit, and painted in the new
more brilliant and fine technique. The 'Master E. S.'
introduced at second-hand the new individualism into
an art quite ready to receive it. There was plenty of
strength in the old German work, but it was of a
blundering and careless kind. The influence of
Flanders turned German workmen into artists, and
enabled them to discipline and direct their powers.
All the delicacy in this print comes from Flanders.
The attempt to give each face an individual expression is Flemish. Whatever tenderness can be
observed, as, for example, in the face of the holy
Abbot, descends from the mystic school of the Rhine
valley, whatever ruggedness, from the old German
schools ; but the complete and careful characterization
of such a face as that of the bareheaded pilgrim
holding his hat was the gift of Jan van Eyck and
Roger.

Without pausing over the engravings by the ' Master
E. S.' further than to note that two of them merely
reproduce Roger's compositions, we may at once
turn to the more renowned Martin Schongauer of
Colmar. Little is known of his life, and that little
has resulted from prolonged investigation and discussion. Kaspar Schongauer, a native of Augsburg,
removed to Colmar about the year 1445, and there
settled down as working goldsmith. Shortly after
his arrival a son was born to him and named Martin.

Doubtless, like Dürer, the future artist received his first instruction from his goldsmith father. Whether he likewise learnt the rudiments of painting at Colmar we do not know, but that is also probable. A foundationless report mentions an otherwise unknown artist as his first master. While still a lad he would in the natural course of things go forth for his years of travel, and the Low Countries would as naturally be the goal of his steps. Lambert Lombard distinctly states that he worked under Roger van der Weyden, and nothing could be more likely. His earliest engravings belong to about 1465, when he was twenty years old and probably took up the mastership of his craft. The British Museum possesses two of his drawings dated 1469, one of which belonged to Albrecht Dürer. These drawings show that Martin's style was fully developed when he was twenty-four years of age. We do not know when he settled down at Colmar, but it was probably at the close of his *Wanderjahre*, about 1464 or 1465, just after Roger's death. In 1473 he painted a fine picture of the Virgin before a hedge of roses, still in the Church of S. Martin at Colmar, for which it was painted. It is the only one of his pictures certainly known to us, though a 'Death of the Virgin' in the National Gallery is often confidently ascribed to him, and there are several pictures from his workshop still to be seen in the Museum at

Colmar. His period of activity was short, for he died in 1488 ; nevertheless, besides the many pictures which he certainly painted, and for which he was widely famed, he left no less than one hundred and sixteen engravings done by his own hand.

The influence of Roger van der Weyden is plainer to be seen in Martin Schongauer than in any other German artist. He did not sink his own individuality in that of his master, but he brought an open and impressible mind to the study of the works of the Brussels artist. The portrait of him at Munich shows a thoughtful and gentle personality, though there is a suggestion of possible wildness in the background. The face is of an almost sensual type, yet it contains no look of grossness. There is an aspect of lazy power about the man, who is obviously younger than the late added inscription would suggest. It is a youth who stands before us with smooth rounded cheeks, and a moustache just budding on his upper lip.

A comparison between Schongauer's engraving of the 'Three Kings' and Roger's picture of the same subject at Munich will serve to show the dependence of the one on the other. The engraving is not a copy of the picture, but it is obviously suggested by it. Every figure in the print finds its prototype in the picture. There is a plant, a hat, and a dog in the one where there is a plant, a hat, and a dog in

THE VIRGIN BEFORE A HEDGE OF ROSES. BY MARTIN SCHONGAUER.
Church of St. Martin at Colmar.

the other. Schongauer's dependence upon Roger is complete even to the head of the ox. The engraving is not the work of a copyist but of a pupil, following his master's footsteps, but keeping a stride of his own. The influence of the old wood-carving forms is seen in the print, though it is scarcely discoverable in the picture. The types of the men's faces differ in the two, and there is a reminiscence of Köln in Schongauer's 'Virgin,' independent of the Köln element which Roger also introduced. Notwithstanding these divergencies, a comparison between print and picture will make plain the meaning of the statement that Schongauer was the medium who, by his prints, carried the influence of Roger all over Europe. Of course 'E. S.' had done something of the same kind, but 'E. S.' was not so strongly influenced by Roger, nor did he attain a reputation like Schongauer's. Schongauer was more famous all Europe over than any other Northern artist before the coming of Dürer. Jacob Wimpheling relates that his prints were sold in Italy, Spain, France, England, and other countries. Engraving became a power in his hands. By means of it he, first of all artists, appealed to the desire of possession in the middle classes. Before his day artists had either worked for the rich few or the general public. Now it was possible for them to address the humbler frequenters of fairs and markets. Because Schongauer was the first thus to address the individual all Europe over he made an unprecedented reputation.

As an artist he did not stand behind Roger. He was a better draughtsman of the human figure than his master. His conceptions were more artistic; his compositions were better balanced and built. But Schongauer's interest for us does not lie so much in his works as in the effect he produced on other artists. It was through him that the savage art of South German painters was first tamed. All his contemporaries on the Upper Rhine and in Franconia and Swabia meekly followed his lead. The power which he thus exercised was in the main that which he derived from the Van Eycks through Roger. It was Roger who showed him how to combine the tenderness of the old mystics with the masculine force pleasant to the Teutonic heart. It was from Roger that he borrowed the sweet womanly type which none ever expressed better than he. He retained the old wooden drapery, the lank and awkward forms, which he had been born to consider admirable, and from which Roger was no more free than he. But he learnt to recognize the charm of landscape, to look not so much for brutality and force as for tenderness and grace. He learnt to beautify whatever he touched, and to make each work a work of art. In fact, he learnt a style; and so working upon all this with original mind he broke a way

into a new epoch, and founded a school which was
destined in less than half a century to produce
such splendid kings of art as Burckmair, Dürer, and
Holbein.

Before quitting this too brief glance at Schongauer,
attention may be directed to one more of his prints,
wherein his weakness and his strength are plainly
discoverable. It is the well-known 'Crucifixion.' No
one can fail to notice in it the feeble drawing of the
nude, and the exaggeration, extending to mannerism,
in the broken folds of the drapery. Equally apparent,
on the other hand, is a tenderness of sentiment so
nearly allied to the work of some Italian artists, that
it is not difficult to imagine a trace (especially in the
figure of St. John) of the influence of Perugino, with
whom we know Schongauer to have had some com-
munication. At first sight this might be mistaken
for a revival of the mystic school, but the sentiment
expressed by these figures is the human sentiment
of sorrow. They do not carry us away into an
ideal world. However the print may look, the artist
who made it was striving to depict a historical fact,
clothed in such garments as the folk of his own
day could best understand. The faces are not mere
ideal creations drawn from the unsubstantial world
of dreams, they are the faces of men and women
of definite character.

The art of Schongauer was based upon reality,

and therefore it had a future of development before it. It was not founded upon any passing and restricted phase of religious emotion. It stood nearer to actual humanity than the art of a Meister Wilhelm. The power by which it had been brought into this closer contact with men, the power by which this new art of the Upper Rhine was vivified, was the influence of the Flemings conveyed through the medium of Roger van der Weyden.

It would be interesting to track the course of this Flemish influence through all the parts of Germany to which it penetrated. At Ulm, for example, the painter Hans Schühlein,* who flourished during the last quarter of the fifteenth century, awoke at the touch of Flanders, and laid the foundations of a school whose style was a development from that of Roger. Schühlein was soon surpassed by a younger contemporary, named Bartholomäus Zeitblom, one of the most gifted men of his day, and an original artist. He learnt engraving in Schongauer's studio, and only late in a variegated life turned his attention to painting. But these, after all, are only the minor lights of art-history; we must turn from them to the masters of greater men.

Wolgemut was born at Nürnberg in 1434, and died there at an advanced age in 1519. He enjoyed much fame in his lifetime, but his memory was over-

* See the wings of the high altar of Tiefenbronn Church.

THE NATIVITY. BY BARTHOLOMÄUS ZEITBLOM. *Ulm.*

shadowed by the greater renown of his pupil, Albrecht Dürer. The investigations of students have at length availed to reinstate him in the position that is his due. We possess no authentic life of him, other than that deducible from his works. Doubtless he learnt the rudiments of art in Nürnberg, where a school of decorative artists was at work, borrowing its style, in almost equal parts, from the schools of Köln and Prag. The historically interesting Imhof altar-piece, in the Lorenz Church at Nürnberg, or the wings of the Deichsler altar in the Berlin Museum, show the kind of level attained by the better artists of the local school in the early years of the fifteenth century. Wolgemut's apprenticeship ended, he too went off on the *Wanderschaft*, and probably spent some years in the Rhine valley. He learnt the

VIRGIN AND CHILD. FROM A NÜRNBERG ALTAR-PIECE. *Berlin Museum.*

Q

rudiments of engraving, and his prints enable us to
trace the development of his style. One of the earliest
represents ' Lot and his Daughters,' and is founded
upon some picture of Meister Stephan's School. The
same may be said of a print of the ' Last Supper.'
Two engravings of the martyrdoms of St. Andrew
and St. Bartholomew are copied from wing panels
(at Frankfurt), which formed part of the altar-piece
of St. Lorenz of Köln; whilst a ' St. Ursula and her
Maidens' is taken from a picture similar to one in
the Köln Museum.

A developing artist in mid-fifteenth century was
not likely to remain satisfied with what the decaying
Köln School could teach him. Like his contemporary, Albrecht Dürer the elder, Wolgemut not
improbably spent some time "with the great artists
in the Netherlands." Certain of his prints seem
founded on, to us unknown, Flemish originals.
Others are copied from the rare engravings of that
excellent Flemish artist, the so-called ' Master of
1480.' Now it was that Wolgemut, like ' E. S.' and
Martin Schongauer, learnt the charm of delicate
handling. His figures become more anatomically
correct; he gives charm to the mere grouping of
lines. By degrees he attains technical dexterity
under the educating influence of Flanders. Further
than this, he adopts the Flemish ideals of form. In
all his works it is henceforward plain, that the

memory of Flanders is a governing influence with
him.   From Flemish artists he borrowed the blue
sky, fading down to a white horizon ; from them the

THE NATIVITY. BY MICHAEL WOLGEMUT. *Zwickau.*

blue distances, the green tree-dotted slopes, the foregrounds alive with insect and flower.   They taught
him to love the sheen of water and the light of day.
Moreover, from them he adopted, and was the first

Q 2

to carry to Nürnberg, that method of painting which the Van Eycks perfected, and to which Roger gave currency.

In all these respects Wolgemut depended upon the artists amongst whom Roger was leader, but it need not be affirmed that Roger was his master. Wolgemut may never have been in the Netherlands ; but some one somewhere brought Roger's influence to bear upon him, and he became a new creature in consequence. He next fell within the orbit of Martin Schongauer, and learnt the best-known technique of engraving from him by copying some of his prints so carefully that the copies are scarcely less precious than the originals. When Wolgemut returned to Nürnberg he was a different man from when he left. He brought back with him experience of foreign work, a new style of painting, a new style of engraving, and above all, the new aim of art, the examination and interpretation of nature. With these he laid the foundation of the Nürnberg school. He came home possessed of that ground-work of knowledge which, enlarged upon and extended in new directions by his own original force, made him, in course of time, the only artist in Europe wholly suited to educate Dürer.

Turning lastly from Franconia to Swabia, from Nürnberg to Augsburg, the influence of the Flemings, gathered up into the hand of Roger, and impressed upon the rude but powerful artists of the rising local school, manifests itself again as the directing force which set them upon the road that swiftly led to greatness. Hans Holbein the elder, born about 1460, and Burckmair, born in 1472, were the two Augsburg artists first worthy of individual fame. The traditions of Flanders came to both of them, and modified their artistic development. Later in their careers both felt the influence of the Italian Renascence, and yielded themselves willingly to it, but it was the traditions of Flanders, indirectly conveyed to them, that raised them from the rank of craftsmen-decorators, and made them artists.

Hans Burckmair is said to have been a direct pupil of Schongauer, but seeing that Schongauer died when Burckmair was only sixteen years old, the Colmar artist's influence upon the young painter must have come rather through his works than his personal teaching. Hans Holbein the elder is more likely to have worked in Schongauer's studio, for not only did Schongauer enjoy European reputation, but, being of an Augsburg family, his fame was likely to take hold upon the artists of that city. When, therefore, young Augsburg journeymen went off on the *Wanderschaft*, Colmar was one of the places to which they would certainly bend their steps.

Schongauer's engravings of course influenced many

men with whom he himself never came in contact. They were spread further abroad than any painter's pictures could be. They were cheap, and young students could buy a few for themselves and study them at home as they could not study the good pictures they might happen to see. A visible connection between the style of an old and young painter usually implied at that time a direct personal connection between the two, but it is unsafe to assume any such direct connection between Schongauer and his followers. Michelangelo in his youth copied Schongauer's print of 'St. Anthony tormented by Demons.' Raphael borrowed from another the type of Christ-Child which he employed in one of his earlier Madonnas.* All the German artists, therefore, whose style of design is obviously founded on that of Schongauer, were not necessarily pupils of his, any more than all the painters whose works show Flemish influence were pupils of Roger van der Weyden.

Schongauer's astonishing fame was largely due to the fact that he was the first to come before the public of Europe as the exponent of a process. Engraving had become the important factor in international art. Henceforward local schools could not remain isolated, as was possible before. Roger lived when, all over Germany, there was a tendency

* See Muntz, *Raphael*, 2nd edition, p. 86.

ST. SEBASTIAN. BY HANS HOLBEIN THE ELDER.

towards increased art production. He lived at the centre, and was the recognized head of that northern school which was pre-eminent both in artistic power and technical skill. In the time of his activity, and amongst the artists who surrounded him and formed their style upon his, the new method of engraving and printing from copper-plates was likewise employed and developed as a fine art. Thus Roger's spirit found its way not merely into some dozens of pictures, but into thousands of beautiful works, strewn broadcast over the face of Europe and attracting the attention always bestowed upon novelties.

The greatness of a man often depends more upon his personal fitness to fill a central place already prepared by the circumstances which likewise fashion him, than upon the exceptional largeness of his talents. Few artists produced a visible effect upon so wide an area as Roger van der Weyden; yet he was neither a great artist nor a great man. His pictures possess a certain charm, but they are seldom instinct with any depth of thought or power of imagination. Van Eyck and Memling were both greater artists than Roger, yet he produced a more visible effect than they. Without Van Eyck, Roger would never have risen above mediocrity. All of excellence that there was in him was borrowed from Jan. Yet Van Eyck's art would never have covered Europe and laid the foundation of many schools without Roger, or some one of like character in his place, to give it currency, Roger's weakness and dependence upon others enabled him to mingle together the various factors that were wanted to make a palatable popular art. Painters everywhere could mould the pliant product as they pleased. At Colmar, Nürnberg, Augsburg, Ulm, they made something different of it. There is little similarity between Holbein the younger and Dürer the younger, yet they were only removed from Roger by two generations of artists. If their work be closely inspected and pulled into its constituent parts, some elements will always be found which they owe, through Roger, to the great Van Eycks.

All art, like all human labour, is continuous. One generation carries on what its predecessor began, and there is solidarity between the works of all the generations of mankind that have ever existed. Step by step the powers of men advance. Step by step discoveries are made and the boundary of the undiscovered is pushed back. Each generation must not only add to but preserve the heritage which its forerunners have given to it. For the vases of truth are passed on from hand to hand, and the golden dust must be gathered into them, grain by grain, from the infinite shore.

CHAPTER VII.

HANS MEMLING.

THE names of only two of the great Flemish artists of the fifteenth century can be called generally famous. Few people have never heard of Van Eyck, and to fewer still is the name of Hans Memling altogether unknown. Roger van der Weyden was really a more important personage than his pupil Memling, but his importance is more likely to be evident to an historical student than to a lover of pictures for their own sakes. Roger's works have been much scattered about, and many were for centuries assigned to his famous pupil, so that much of Memling's renown ought by rights to belong to his master. Though, however, Memling's name has never passed through a period of total eclipse, it was for some time partly forgotten, and was preserved only in the misspelt form of Hemling. Moreover, the details of his life fell into oblivion, and a legend was constructed to supply the defect of facts. He was fabled to have been wounded in battle, taken to the hospital of St. John at Bruges, and there nursed and restored to health, in return for which charity he painted the pictures to the possession of which that institution now owes its world-wide fame. The falsity of this little tale has been revealed by the labours of modern investigators, and the true frame-work of the artist's life has been rediscovered. It seems likely that he was by birth a German, born about the year 1430. Where he spent the first part of his life we do not know. It is alone evident that at some time he came directly under the influence of Roger van der Weyden, for not only did he adopt that painter's types even for individual figures, but the existence of one picture is recorded, of which the centre panel was painted by Roger and the wings by Memling—a combination easily explained if Memling was at that time a workman in Roger's employ. It is not, however, till Memling was over thirty years of age that we get any certain knowledge about him.

His earliest authentic picture now known is the altar-piece belonging to the Duke of Devonshire. It represents Sir John Donne with his wife and daughter kneeling before the Virgin and Child. It must have been painted after 1461, because the Knight and his lady wear the collar of the livery of the Rose and Sun, an order instituted in that year. It was probably painted before 1466, because only a daughter is represented, whereas in that year a son was born. It was at all events painted before 1469, the year of the Knight's death.* Thus between 1461 and 1466 Memling emerges upon the scene as an artist, and an artist already in the full enjoyment of his powers. Where he was then residing we do not know. The picture may have been painted in England; we have no proof to the contrary. On the left wing, bearing a representation of John Baptist, the artist's patron saint, he has introduced into the background what must be a portrait of himself in his working attire. An anonymous Italian writer of the sixteenth century describing a no longer extant portrait of Memling by himself, says that it depicts a " man rather stout than otherwise, and of a ruddy complexion." Such is the build and appearance of the workman in this wing. He seems, moreover, to be thirty-two or thirty-three years of age, which is about what he ought to have been at the time in question.†

In the year 1478 we know from documentary evidence that Memling had already been long resident at Bruges. He continued to reside there up to

* Brighton Art Loan Exhibition of 1884, Catalogue.
† Mr. Weale has called attention to an etching after one of Memling's numerous pictures of his patron saint, John the Baptist, upon which it is stated in an old handwriting that this is a portrait of Memling by himself. The character of the artist is, however, so plainly visible in his work, and is so totally different from the character of this meagre, hairy enthusiast, that the attribution cannot be accepted.

the time of his death in 1495. Bruges was the city
where all his best work was done, and with it, in the
days of its highest glory and wealth, his name is
inseparably coupled. It is impossible now to pass in
review all or even most of Memling's chief existing
works. He was probably a more prolific painter in
oil than any of his predecessors. Jan van Eyck was
slow by disposition, and moreover the Flemish system
of oil painting was new in his hands. Roger van der
Weyden developed a more rapid technique, but the
development must itself have been a work of time.
Memling inherited the labours of his predecessors,
and was thus enabled to work faster than they, whilst
at the same time attaining at any rate as perfect
a degree of finish as Roger. In one respect Memling
differed greatly from Jan van Eyck; he laid less
stress upon light and shade. His pictures are all
illuminated by an equable light, seldom rising to
great brightness, and never sinking to strong shadow.
He did not aim at the same perfect rendering of
solid form by means of shade. This made his task
simpler, for he had more spaces of flat colour to deal
with, and he avoided the necessity of carefully working out solid forms from point to point. Memling's
pictures charm us rather by their harmony of colour
and grace of outline than by their distribution of
light and shade. His work being thus simplified
he was able to paint faster, and, besides, he did not

endeavour to introduce the same multitude of details. So he made more pictures even than Roger, and from amongst them a tolerably large number survive in more or less perfect condition.

Instead, therefore, of glancing hastily at many of his works, it will be better to consider rather what was his quality and position as an artist both individually and in relation to his fellows, turning, as we want them, to those of his paintings which best express his several gifts and weaknesses.

The most finished, the best designed, and the most famous of his works is the little shrine of St. Ursula in the Hospital of St. John at Bruges,* into which the relics of the Saint were removed in the year 1489. All the wonderful story of the Saint's life was painted on six panels, three on each side of the shrine. It so happens that just about the same time (1490-95) Carpaccio was likewise painting† in Venice the same beautiful tale, and a comparison between the work of these two men is of the highest interest, and will serve to manifest some of Memling's most remarkable characteristics.

Carpaccio in the main chooses courtly and ceremonial incidents from the legend for the subjects of his pictures—the sending and receiving of ambassadors and the like—all of them events happening in cities which are so many repetitions of the artist's

* Phot. Braun and Nohring.   † Phot. Naya.

own Venice. The finest and most deservedly popular of the series is the picture in which the angel of God appears as a dream to St. Ursula while she sleeps in her own little bed. There are but two figures in the picture—the rest of the space is occupied by the interior of the bed-room, wherein, like Faust in Gretchen's chamber, you may trace the sweet influences of the maiden owner by the little things she has left about : the little desk with its hour-glass, the shelf or two of books, the slippers by the bed-side, the shrine and basin of holy water on the wall, and the plants in pots on the sill of the latticed window. The angel bearing a palm branch, the bright promise of the crown of martyrdom, enters gently with the dawn light at the door. Maid Ursula herself is the very incarnation of peace. She has slept the long night through so still, with her face resting on her little hand, that the bed-clothes are not disturbed by one uneven fold. There is no restlessness in her nature. Her face is unutterably calm and sweet— the face of one over whom the years have passed without one ruffling touch. Nor indeed could aught ruffle her gentle heart, for peace abides in her. The promise of a violent death comes thus, and without a movement of the slumberer is thus received. The subject was altogether suited to Carpaccio's heart. He painted it with delight. The picture is his master-piece. For Memling, on the contrary, it is a subject of small importance, a very minor incident. He only introduces it into the background of one of his panels—paints the angel flying in a great hurry into Ursula's bedroom, and the awakened saint sitting bolt upright in bed in an attitude of obedient attention. The charm of the legend for Memling lay in its character as a tale of adventure. Norseman-like, the idea of these eleven thousand travelling virgins pleased him by its quaintness, by its resemblance to a fairy tale. He only chose five subjects for his six panels, three of them being incidents on the voyage up the Rhine, one the reception of the pilgrim multitude by the Pope, and one the martyrdom of the entire company. The whole tale is, to the painter, a romance full of incident. He wishes in telling it in his pictures to attract attention to the facts as he knows them. Moreover, by preference he chooses incidents which happened in the country. Cities are his background—in three cases the city of Köln painted from sketches made on the spot ; but always he pictures his young saintesses at the outskirts of the town. The open air and the strong-flowing river are the scenes he loves best.

Memling indeed always loved water, and especially flowing water ; he introduces it whenever possible into the background of his pictures. Often it is a stream turning a mill-wheel ; sometimes it is a brook crossed by a wooden bridge ; sometimes a lazy river

R

brightened with snowy swans.   He was the first man,
so far as I know, who ever drew the form of a river-
bank correctly, and it is clear that much of his time
at one period of his life must have been passed in an
undulating country watered by fair streams—such a
country, indeed, as is to be found up the Rhine a
few miles above Köln.   But if Memling possessed a
northerner's love of incident and adventure, it was in
a different spirit from the poets of the Edda.   What
was wild and weird had no more charms for him than
for his Venetian contemporary.   His character was
not in sympathy with strength but with purity.   He
never painted a stormy sky or a rugged landscape,
but only smiling meadows under the evening sunlight of a summer day.   The fairy tale attracted him
rather than the hero song.   The simple adventures of
errant maidens were his theme, not the hazardous
wanderings of armed knights.   It seems strange that
the sturdy burghers of Flanders, phlegmatic in peace
and fiery in war as they often proved themselves,
should have found pleasure in idyllic works of art,
rather than in more soul-exciting subjects.   Yet
such was the case.   A few centuries had removed
them very far away in thought from the savage ideals
of their forefathers ; the great age of monks and nuns
and mendicant saints had left its mark upon them,
and now, just at the eve of the Reformation, the artist
of their choice paints on the shrine for the supposed

bones of an unreal saint a fairy tale enshrining the scarcely believed relics of an ancient faith.

How thoroughly the spirit of a fairy tale reigns in these pictures, one has but to glance at them to see. The eleven thousand virgins of English noble birth, all bareheaded and clothed in the rich costumes of the fifteenth-century Burgundian court, go sailing up the Rhine, tightly packed together in little boats. There is something of Flemish literalness in it all, and yet it is a literalness of a fanciful kind. Each scene looks like a picnic. There is the real Köln in the background, the ship (a real ship) at the quay, and twelve young ladies landing on the shore. But for the presence of an angel in the background, we should not have supposed that anything miraculous was intended. It is in the sudden changes, the surprising succession of events, that the fairy element comes in, just as in any other fairy tale where the fascination lies in rapid changes of scene and circumstance by supernatural agency, though each individual incident, taken alone, may be perfectly natural and ordinary. Princesses and milkmaids are common enough mortals, but the sudden elevation of a milkmaid to be a princess, the sudden transformation of surroundings and attire, is the surprising work of the fairies, and the charm of the tale lies in the surprise. Even so is it with Memling's pictured tale. In one panel you see the pretty

R 2

company landing at Basle, and without a moment's
pause starting off one after another along the road
to Rome, each so wrapped up in her own thoughts
that no two walk together side by side. They step
along daintily with the skirts of their pretty dresses
held carefully up. Then comes the magic transformation. In the next panel the four or five hundred
miles of journey, with its alpine fastnesses, its forests,
and its dangers of every kind, have been safely
accomplished without fatigue, and we find ourselves
in Rome, watching the arrival of the un-travel-stained
company. Along the level country road, in through
the gate, and up the street of the city, they come
to the portal of a church, where the Pope and his
cardinals are assembled to receive them, whilst at
the same moment Prince Conon, Ursula's betrothed,
likewise arrives with his knights, and all joyfully
receive baptism together at the hands of the priests.
We do not see them again until the time of their
departure from Basle in company with Pope, bishops,
and cardinals on their return journey. The picture
is of exceeding beauty,—the little ship packed with
such well-dressed and gently-demeanoured personages,
the Pope seated in the midst, radiant of countenance,
and pouring forth words of holy wisdom, to which
the devout company pay reverent and delighted
attention. The remaining two panels contain the
martyrdom : in the first of them the maidens are

St. Ursula received by the Pope. By Hans Memling. *Bruges.*

being shot down and Prince Conon dies in the arms
of his bride; the other panel is reserved for the
death of the glorious Ursula alone. But these
martyrdom pictures are quite unreal. The soldiers
are perfect gentlemen. Their chiefs look on with
smiling wonder and a kind of reverent delight. The
beholder, at a first glance, may receive some notion
of violence and the like, but another look is re-
assuring. Clearly no harm is being done; it is only
a pantomime. The soldiers, who look as though they
were shooting arrows at the maidens, soon win our
confidence. For all their acting, their eyes betray
them, and we trust them instinctively. From a hasty
glance we might think the girls in the boat were
being killed, but we soon see that they are not; they
throw their arms about and shrink behind the gun-
wale as if they were frightened; but they are bad
actresses; we see through it all at once, and the
innocent deception raises a smile.

The same spirit manifests itself in all Memling's
treatments of miraculous subjects, as for example, in
the charming panel at Munich, for which the 'Light
of the World'* has been suggested as a name,
though even that is not satisfactory. The picture is
a work of the old school, in that it is a kind of
painted chronicle, the several incidents being introduced together, artificially separated one from

* Phot. Hanfstaengl.

another by buildings, walls, or mounds of earth. The subjects represented begin with the Annunciation, the *Gloria in Excelsis*, and the Nativity ; then follows the whole story of the Coming, Adoration, and Departure of the Magi, the Flight into Egypt, and Massacre of the Innocents. The remainder of the picture is devoted to incidents in the Christian story following upon the Resurrection. First the Resurrection itself, then Christ as the Gardener, Christ on the way to Emmaus, Christ appearing to the Virgin, and again His appearance to the fishing disciples ; the Ascension, Pentecost, and the Death and Assumption of the Virgin bring the tale to an end. For such a work the old name, 'The Seven Joys of the Virgin,' seems as good as any. The central incident in the foreground is the 'Adoration of the Magi,' and the greater part of the background is devoted to the journey of the kings, all the chief incidents of which are related in succession. Away in the farthest distance the three wise men, standing each on the summit of a mountain, behold with wonder the miraculous star. Seized alike with the desire to find the new-born King of whose advent they are thus made aware, they start upon their several journeys, each with a company of mounted followers. They accidentally meet together at a bridge where their three roads converge. Presently they are seen again, saluting Herod in the courtyard of the palace, whilst a few yards farther on the Jewish monarch appears taking counsel with his advisers. The cavalcade comes into sight again in the foreground, and at length the far-travelled kings kneel in adoration before the Babe of their search. Their stay is but brief, and we soon behold the gay company riding away along another road, which brings them to the shore of a calm land-locked lagoon, where three ships await them, embarking upon which, each king with his men, they sail peacefully homeward along the waters towards the half-buried sun in the west.

However little this grouping together of the incidents may please the fastidious taste of a scientific age, the picturing of the incidents themselves cannot fail to call forth praise. They are painted, like the incidents in the Ursula series, with an excellent story-telling faculty. If we except the three kings on the tops of their hills, all the miraculous parts of the legend are left out for the spectator to supply from his memory. Those incidents only are chosen which lend themselves to pictorial treatment, and few pieces of Flemish landscape are better than the view of the lagoon with the three vessels dropping gently down the tide into the golden sunset. But the most charming parts of the panel illustrate two of the early incidents relative to the life of Christ. The first is the apparition of the angel to the

shepherds. The flock of snow-white sheep are grazing
all around upon a hill-top, whilst their three simple-
hearted guardians sit or lean upon the grass, one
of them playing a bagpipes for the diversion of the
rest. Just then the white-robed messenger of heaven
appears gently before them. There is no hurry or
flutter about him, nor is there any sign of fright in
the men. The piper stops his tune, though without
taking his fingers from the pipes or rising from the
ground. All three listen with rapt attention, and
the angel speaks his message with a quiet and gentle
earnestness.

Sweeter still, though almost invisible because so far
away in the distance (in the upper left-hand corner),
is the little picture of the 'Flight into Egypt.' The
road along which the travellers must go winds among
undulating meadows and leafy copses. Already the
morning portion of the way has been accomplished;
it is the hour of rest. The ass is unsaddled and
turned adrift to graze according to his will; Joseph
has gone aside to fetch water from a fountain, whilst
the Virgin and Child rest under a date tree, which
bends down to them of itself and offers them its
ripe fruit. It is a little idyl that a poet might have
sung. The same subject has been painted with
some frequency, but nowhere is the beauty of it so
sweetly or so simply shown as here.

Memling excelled in painting such religious fairy

tales. He was not in reality a religious artist. None of his pictures give evidence of any passionate faith or enthusiasm such as animated the old artists of Köln. Nor does he ever succeed in representing any of the grander Scriptural conceptions. A favourite subject of fifteenth and early sixteenth century artists, for example, was the Apocalyptic poem. So popular was it that, even before the introduction of movable types, one of the first books ever printed was an illustrated Apocalypse, which ran through several editions we know of, and doubtless many that have not come down to us. Dürer also, almost during the lifetime of Memling, published such a set of prints—the finest work of wood-cutting up to that time made, and the finest pictures of the poem made at any time. His great and strong imagination entered into the exalted and mystic spirit of the poem, and his hand expressed it with rough and resistless energy. For the wing of his most famous triptych * Memling had to handle the same subject, and he did it conscientiously, as he did everything he put his hand to ; but it was not a work of love, and this part of the picture was not a success. Symbolic stones fall flaming into a real sea, devils and dragons perform their appointed tasks, but the whole thing is dead. The subjects have not been grasped by the painter's imagination, and do not come forth hot from the deep of his soul. Even the

* At Bruges.

four riders, who were often pictured with great power by northern artists, are here nothing but strangely bedizened men, galloping furiously along islands little larger than the horses they ride. The feebleness of invention in this part of the picture becomes all the more apparent by contrast with the noble figure of St. John seated in the foreground, beholding and writing down his vision of wonder. Not that he is the John a reader of the Apocalypse would be likely to imagine, or indeed one that a person to whom the poem was well known and well understood would be apt to admire. There is indeed an earnestness and solemnity in the face, but it lacks fire and force of character. Nevertheless, the conception of the man as one beholding, with reverent and long-continued attention, marvellous sights, to him alone revealed, is certainly fine. The gentle and observant mind in him is full on the stretch, his eye seems to be endeavouring to penetrate still further, to be watching so as to miss nothing of the swiftly-changing vision. On his lap is a parchment volume wherein he writes with the implements of a professional scribe, St. John being the patron of the illuminators' guild at Bruges.

Jan van Eyck was a man of fact, his work is an attempt to state the uttermost truth about things. He loved to elaborate their solid shape with perfect veracity. In his pictures light and shade, texture, colour, and outline, have about equal stress laid upon

them. In this respect he is one of the most complete
of artists. Roger van der Weyden in his turn cared
less about solid form, and less about light and shade.
He laid chief stress upon outlines, striving to make
them graceful so far as in him lay. Hugo van der
Goes was neither a colourist nor a great delineator.
He was a man of passion, desirous of producing great
and striking effects. He therefore laid emphasis
upon light and shade, as all passionate artists are
inevitably led to do. Memling was neither passionate
like Hugo, nor earnest like Jan van Eyck. He was
formed of milder stuff. In his pictures, therefore, no
stress is laid upon shadow, neither is he a colourist
in the proper sense of the term. The people of his
dreams were dwellers in a land where "there is light
alike by day and alike by night." They did not tread
the work-a-day world betwixt glare of sunshine and
gloom of cloud. The heavens over their head are
ever clear, a perpetual evening light fills the air.
It is a land "in which it seemeth always afternoon,"
a place like

> "the island-valley of Avillon,
> Where falls not hail, or rain, or any snow,
> Nor ever wind blows loudly ; but it lies
> Deep meadowed, happy, fair with orchard lawns
> And bowery hollow crowned with summer sea."

It is in fact the country of the heavenly Jerusalem,
which " had no need of the sun, neither of the moon,

to shine in it, for the glory of God did lighten it, and the Lamb is the light thereof." Now and again indeed Memling hankers after a little brilliancy, as when he would paint a star above the cradle of the Child, or would illumine the airy pathway of the ascending Christ. Yet even in these cases he flies to gilding for refuge; he will not purchase light by shadow—the only sacrifice whereby it can be attained. All this is in perfect keeping with the general drift of his art. He was a painter of fairy tales, not of facts. The world seen through his eyes assumed mellower tones. He beheld not men of violence; he loved not the iron-handed. His ideal was the Prince of Peace. Thus Memling returned at one time even nearer to the old religious ideal of the artists of Köln than his master had done. In one or two cases, notably in the St. Ursula series, which may have been painted after a journey to the capital city of the Lower Rhine, he paints Madonnas and Saints unmistakably suggested by pictures of Meister Wilhelm's school. But the times were no longer what they had been. Roger van der Weyden had gone exactly far enough in that direction, he had carried along with him the whole body of northern artists, and formed the most powerful school of the century in the north of Europe. Memling did not attain the same influence. His own pictures were popular, he had his due share, and perhaps more than his due share, of pupils, but he did not found a school as Roger had done, and did not even restrain to any perceptible degree the decline of that school after Roger's death. The new tendencies became yearly stronger. A generation more was to see the transfer of the centre of art-life in the north from Flanders to Franconia. Dürer was about to come to the front and lead all his contemporaries in willing thraldom. Memling was to be succeeded by Patenier, Lucas van Leyden, and Quentin Massys, every one of them men of a new cast of thought, men to whom the ideals of Memling were nothing but a dream from which they were glad to be awakened.

In spite of his naturally mediæval cast mind, it was, however, impossible for Memling in those rapidly advancing days not to be in some degree carried away. In the last years of his life, and especially in his last picture, the 'Crucifixion' at Lübeck,* he begins to show plainly the influence produced upon him. He there strives after that greater energy of expression which was foreign to his own nature, but which the taste of the day began to demand ; and curiously enough, at the same time that he takes this step, he harks back more plainly than in any other picture to the work of his master Roger, frankly borrowing from his 'Descent from the Cross' one entire figure and the suggestion for three more.

* Phot. Nohring. Chromolith. Arundel.

This conservation of individual figures is one of Memling's frequent habits. He was not creative in the sense that Dürer and Tintoret were creative. Both of those geniuses seem to have so overflowed with ideas that life was not long enough, as Dürer expressly tells us, to give form to a tithe of them. Memling, like several of his contemporaries, adhered in the main to a certain not inconsiderable number of figures, which he painted again and again in different combinations. All the subjects given him were of a certain type and class, and the actors suited for one set of parts were suited for all the rest. To take one example, where many might be cited, Memling makes continual use of the same angel in several of his 'Madonna' pictures. It is a smiling angel, sometimes playing on an organ, but usually offering to the Child an apple, type of the sin which He was born to take away. This angel appears first in the Duke of Devonshire's picture of the Virgin with Sir John Donne. It comes again in the Belvedere 'Madonna,' * in the Uffizi 'Madonna,' † in a 'Madonna' at Wörlitz, in the St. Catherine altar-piece at Bruges, and I believe in the 'Madonna' which perished at Strassburg during the Franco-German War. The original of the type was borrowed from Van Eyck, and may be found on the Ghent altar-piece, and again on the outside of the little altar-

* Phot. Miethke and Wawra.   † Phot. Alinari.

piece at Dresden,* where it was probably painted by a pupil. This is sufficient to show that Memling was not an original artist. In almost every one of his pictures there are strong reminiscences of Roger van der Weyden, indeed Memling the artist was Roger's greatest work. He was not original, he had to be taught every word and phrase of the language he was to employ. Once taught it he scarcely modified it at all ; he did what was better, he used it. He told the pretty tales that were given him, and made them prettier in the telling. He brought forth secret things of great price by the magic he had not invented but acquired. His was not the very greatest work, but it was honest and of value.

One of the chief secrets of Memling's success was that he knew the limits of his powers. There is the same absence of ambition in him as in Fra Angelico. He gave more pains to the designing of things than the Florentine friar, but it was pains of a humble kind. He was not on the search after novelty. He took the art of the day as he found it, worked to the best of his power according to the rules he had been taught, yielded without obstinacy to whatever influences were brought to bear upon him, and so by degrees attained greater certainty and facility of hand. But he never tried to effect anything beyond

* Berlin Phot. Co.

S

his powers. He did not waste his energies in struggling after what to him must ever have remained unattainable. With such a temperament alone was work possible of the kind he produced. The atmosphere of peace is breathed throughout it. To lose oneself in a picture of his is to take a pleasant and healthy rest. The struggling world is exchanged for a world of gentleness and peace. It has not been given to many men to leave so rich a heritage. Memling's success is fraught with a lesson not for artists alone. Moreover, because Memling always kept within his powers, we hardly perceive, except after much seeking, what the limits of those powers were. It is by his failures that a man shows the boundary between what he can do and what he cannot. One who never fails appears greater than a more powerful artist who fails continually because he tries to attain what is beyond his reach. The works of a man of many struggles may possess elements of grandeur and present effects that surprise, but they cannot be instinct with peace. One to whom peace is the breath of his art-life must, by the nature of things, be humble and obedient, drawing from others the knowledge which can only be attained first of all by a struggle, and reaping the reward which his predecessors and contemporaries have sown, and of which they have been unable, or only partly able, to garner in the fruits.

From the days of Van Eyck onwards portrait painting had formed a large part of every good artist's work.
Jan van Eyck was employed by the people about the
Burgundian court to paint their likenesses with perfect
frankness. A few of them wanted to be in the
proximity of the Madonna, but for the most part, not
without the painter's visible approval, they were satisfied to be depicted alone. Roger van der Weyden
quickly adapted himself to the twofold requirements
of the day. For pious folk he painted the religious
altar-pieces they wanted, and introduced portraits of
the devout donors in the proper places. But he also
executed with like skill a number of single portraits,
and in this branch of art likewise set the fashion afterwards followed. Every one of Jan van Eyck's
portraits is wholly different from every other. The
pictures are all as characteristically individual as the
persons portrayed. In Roger's portraits, on the contrary, there is a greater similarity. He looked at all
men from a more subjective point of view, and instead
of losing himself in them, he comprehended them in
himself. Thus all Roger's portraits bear the stamp of
his own cast of mind upon their faces. Moreover,
they are done in a way that could be imitated. They
catch the expression of the sitter, but pass over
detailed marks of character. No one who had not
the insight, the patience, and the richly-endowed
artistic nature of Van Eyck could have made such

S 2

portraits as he made. But these qualities were not transferable. A school of portrait painters of that fibre could not arise. Roger's method of portrait painting, on the contrary, could be taught and learnt. Hence it came to pass that a great many portraits exist bearing more or less the characteristic marks of Roger's treatment and commonly assigned to his hand, but in reality the work of pupils of his school. Memling's single portraits now remaining are of this kind; but they are only five in number. His patrons seem to have been mostly pious people. Worldly-minded folk went to other artists for what they wanted. A man who wanted an altar-piece was well advised to go to Memling. Thus it comes to pass that most of Memling's portraits are either included in the midst of heavenly and saintly personages, or they form at least the halves of diptychs, the other halves consisting of a Madonna or a patron saint. The best of such diptychs is the Madonna with Martin van Newenhoven, in the Academy of Bruges. There is another, an unknown man with St. Benedict, in the Uffizi at Florence,* but this has been divided into two parts which came to be considered separate pictures. Perhaps some of Memling's other portraits are like-wise parts of divided diptychs, and if so the number of single figures might be still further reduced. Certain it is, at any rate, that Memling painted a man better

* Phot. Alinari.

in an attitude of devotion than anyhow else. Not
that he gave him much fervour of expression, but he
was thus enabled to bring him harmoniously into
that somewhat unreal atmosphere of peace in which
his imagination was alone free to range. Portraits by
Memling, included in altar-pieces, exist in such
quantity that it is difficult to choose from amongst
them any one as typical of the rest. In the 'Madonna
with St. George,' * belonging to the National Gallery,
there is a rather uninteresting kneeling donor. The
Duchatel 'Madonna' † in the Louvre contains the
portraits of a father and mother, with their seven sons
and twelve daughters, kneeling before the Virgin's
throne. Compared to Van Eyck's or Hugo's portraits,
there is in these one and twenty people a remarkable
lack of individuality. The lack indeed is more apparent
at the first glance than it becomes upon a closer in-
spection. Memling's personality hangs like a veil
between the beholder and the persons portrayed. The
veil is least obscure on the side of the women. Their
individual characters, though all cast in similar moulds,
can be traced with tolerable ease. The little boys also
in the background were evidently pleasant objects to
the artist, and he painted them with care and brought
out their boyishness distinctly. But the strong and
frowning father was not much to his liking, and he
set him down carefully but with little love.

* Berlin Phot. Co. and Braun.   † Phot. Braun.

A family of parents, boys, and girls are likewise
portrayed upon the wings of the St. Christofer altar-
piece at Bruges. The father was by name Willem
Moreel, a special patron and friend of Memling's.
Not only did he order this large altar-piece of the
painter, but at other times he caused him to paint
the three separate portraits of himself, his wife, and
one of his daughters. Moreel, or Morelli, as his
name should be, was the descendant of a Savoyard
family long resident in Bruges. He had a large
connection with Italian merchants, was at the head
of a banking establishment called the Bank of Rome,
and was one of the wealthiest inhabitants of Bruges.
About him personally we know little more than that
he was a successful man of business. Memling paints
him as an artist would who knew his face well; he
catches his bright, capable expression, and the peculiar position of the lips which indicate the strength
of his will. It is the only strong-willed face in any
of Memling's pictures. The lads behind him have
the vivacity of their father, but no trace of his force
of character yet visible on their faces. The girls are
all one much like another; if you look carefully you
can see their little individualities peeping out; but
the painter's ideal of feminine sweetness (never better
incorporated than in the St. Barbera standing behind) is
more or less seen by him in every woman's face, and
thus his insight into individual character is crippled.

MARTIN VAN NEWENHOVEN. BY HANS MEMLING. *Bruges.*

Unquestionably the finest of Memling's portraits is, however, none of these, but the half-length figure of Martin van Newenhoven in an attitude of devotion before the Madonna. The man himself is no very superb specimen of humanity; he has a bright and pleasant though rather foolish face; but such as he is Memling has caught the idea of him, and placed him visibly and knowably on the panel. Further, he has not only made a likeness but a picture of him, and a fine picture too. Its colouring is unusual and most beautiful. The textures of the garments are superb, and not only are the little landscapes seen through the open windows full of the charm that Memling always threw into his backgrounds, but the charm extends to the interior of the room, with its stained glass windows, panelled walls, looking-glass, and other pieces of furniture. This patient elaboration of the interior is, doubtless, due to the fact that Memling had recently seen and admired Jan van Eyck's portrait of the Arnolfini, which was at Bruges. That both pictures have a convex mirror on the farthest wall, reflecting the backs of the persons whose faces are turned to the beholder, is no mere coincidence.

The Virgin here, though beautiful, is not superior to several of Memling's other Madonnas. The Child is inferior to most. Of all Flemish painters, except perhaps David, Memling was by nature best disposed for painting infants. In this branch of art we have

to go to Italy for the finest work. The Italians had
an inborn and national delight in the fairness and
sweetness of womanhood and infancy. So far as I
know, there is only one really superb picture of an
infant in the world painted by a northern artist up
to the time of Reynolds, and that is a child Christ
by Dürer in the Uffizi at Florence. Even it is not a
generally attractive picture, but for perfect sympathy
with the weakness, the tenderness, and the mystery
of babyhood it has no parallel in the world. The
new-born babe in Hugo's 'Nativity' comes next, not
in attractiveness, for it is hideous, but in veracity.
Jan van Eyck carried the ugliness of his children to
an extreme, and in labouring at details which he had
not sympathy to unite nor tenderness rightly to
understand, he produced a series of diminutive old
men which are more hideous than can well be
imagined. Of Memling's children two at least are
of a high order of merit—the child Christ on the lap
of the Virgin in the St. Catherine altar at Bruges
and the Christ borne by St. Christofer in Moreel's
picture in the same town. The former is a genuine
baby, and is by all means the best of the two ; He
has that look of uncertainty in the management of
His little limbs which is the peculiar fascination in a
child, whilst at the same time He possesses the graces
of soft and rounded forms which only little children
can own. The other Child is older, and already a

man in gesture and expression; but, regard being
had to the legend of St. Christofer, His appearance
is just what it should be. For here He is not the
Child of the sacred history, but a visionary re-incarn-
ation come down for a moment to reward the saint's
charity. A child, it is related, came one night to his
hut (at the edge of a ford, across which he was wont
to carry travellers for the service of God), and prayed
to be taken across in the storm. As he went, the
waters rose higher, and the child became heavier, and
the strong man was puzzled, and hard put to to come
to the other side. Nevertheless he came safely forth,
and then the child revealed to him that he was
his master Christ, and so vanished away. At the
moment chosen by the painter the saint is looking
up, wondering at the weight of his strange burden,
and the child, holding on to his hair with one hand,
and blessing with the other, is smiling at the wonder
of his gigantic bearer. The tale, were there but
space to tell it at length, is one of the most beautiful
of mediæval legends, and it has seldom been better
rendered into painting than here.

The picture is by some held to be Memling's
masterpiece, and parts of it indeed are excellent, but
it was not by a work of this class that the artist's full
powers could be brought out. Gentle, cordial, affec-
tionate, humble, painstaking as Memling must have
been, his best works are those of the St. Ursula series

type, where his fancy could play about bright and
fairy-like creatures, where no storm nor the memory
of a storm need ever come, where no clouds darkened
the sky, and not even the brilliant tones of sunset
gave forecast of a coming night. Such a man as
Memling could never found a school, or flourish in
spite of opposition and neglect, but, born at a time
ripe for his coming, growing up under the tutelage
provided just at the right moment for him, he was
enabled to climb almost without difficulty to the
highest level attained by contemporary artists.

CHAPTER VIII.

THE RISE OF LANDSCAPE PAINTING.

PAINTERS of what we had best go on calling the Gothic period, that is to say, of the twelfth, thirteenth, and fourteenth centuries, aimed at suggesting thoughts to the beholder of their pictures, not at presenting visible facts. They tried to take him up to heaven and show him the everlasting hierarchies, the immortal saints, and the personified powers of life. Thus they were not compelled to employ the similitudes of all the objects of nature, but only those which the use and wont of preachers, poets, and theologians had fastened upon as specially emblematical of heavenly things. Their works, moreover, were intended to serve as architectural decorations, and so had to be painted under severe restrictions. In the National Gallery there hangs a late Venetian picture representing a great procession going past the Scuola di San Rocco on a gala day. The exterior of the Scuola and its neighbouring houses is adorned with a number of oil-paintings resting upon carved mouldings or fastened to pillars. A glance at the picture is sufficient to show how utterly the ordinary oil-painting fails when employed as an architectural embellishment. Pictures which are to adorn and form part of a building, especially a building of the Gothic type, must consist of figures, separated one from another, all standing in simple and restful attitudes, and all plainly relieved against a light ground. The Gothic artists understood this, and their pictures (excepting of course merely decorative patterns) were painted with plain or gilt backgrounds. The gold background is the rule in early panel pictures and miniatures. In elaborate works it was covered with diaper patterns inwrought with colours, and the figures usually stood upon tesselated or plain pavements.

The first sign of a closer approach to inanimate nature appeared in the introduction of flowers. The songs of the knightly poets were full of the joy of spring, of the flowery meadows, the green trees, and the clear sky. The climate of heaven was pictured as thus ever fair—fields lit by the Sun of Righteousness and carpeted with unfading flowers. Thus the Virgin and Saints in the fourteenth century were usually depicted by the painters of Köln standing or seated upon flowery turf, the rest of the background being still of burnished gold. The flowers were painted individually with perfect veracity and love, and none of the Van Huysems and Van Os's of later schools ever caught the sentiment of the stars of the field as their scorned predecessors of a forgotten day had done.

It was not until the centre of the art-life of Northern Europe was shifted by the powerful impulse of the Van Eycks to the Low Countries, that the element of landscape became important in works of painting. The 'Adoration of the Lamb' is the first picture with a fine landscape background. The veracity of Jan van Eyck led him to look at nature in the same objective fashion as he looked at man. He took things as they are, little and great together, and thought no more scorn to spend his time in fixing the lineaments of a floating cloud than in tracing the outlines of a human lip. Between the landscape background painted by Jan van Eyck in 1432 and the landscapes with figures painted by Gerard David and Joachim de Patenier, in the early years of the following century, lies the development now to be traced.

Jan van Eyck we know was a traveller ; even if we had not known it otherwise, his pictures would acquaint us with the fact. The palm trees, clear skies, and snowy mountains in the background of the 'Adoration of the Lamb' never flourished in the flats of Flanders, yet they have been painted from nature direct by the help of an observant eye. It is

curious that, so far as I know, Jan did not introduce
the likenesses or costumes of foreigners into his
pictures. The prophets and sages of old time in the
'Adoration' are indeed dressed in strange attire and
wear outlandish head-gear, but the artist invented
those himself; he did not even go on to the quays of
Bruges for a suggestion, still less did he bring home
from Portugal a sketch-book full of costumes and
types of face, such as Dürer made on his famous
journey. We shall not be far wrong in concluding
that upon his travels Jan van Eyck's eye was open
rather to nature than to men. It must have been so,
for no one could have brought into art at a bound, as
he did, an entirely or almost entirely new factor
unless it had possessed the strongest attractions for
him. Jan van Eyck is then to be remembered not
only as the co-inventor of a new system of painting
and the originator of the great school of portraiture,
but also as the founder of modern landscape art. In
the whole range of art history no other so truly
original a master can be found. Even Dürer falls
behind him in this respect, and of the Italians there is
not one to equal him, not even Giotto or Masaccio.

Of Jan van Eyck's landscapes four examples shall
be taken, all being backgrounds to figure pictures.
The most important is that on the central and lower
wing panels of the 'Adoration of the Lamb'; after
these come the 'Madonna with Chancellor Rollin' at

the Louvre, the 'St. Francis receiving the Stigmata' at Turin, and the drawing of 'St. Barbera' at Antwerp. They are examples of four kinds of landscape. In the 'Adoration' we have a cultivated garden, in the 'Rollin Madonna' a view from a window overlooking a city with snow-covered mountains in the very far distance, in the 'St. Francis' a bit of rocky wilderness by a river near a town, and in the 'St. Barbera' a hillside draped with fields and dotted with trees along the hedges. The landscape of heaven is of course the picture of a dream, and though in all its details founded upon minute study of nature, is not the reflection of any particular spot. The other three examples are evidently taken direct from nature; indeed, in the case of the 'Rollin Madonna,' Mr. Weale has identified the town in the background as Maastricht. The same qualities that Jan brought to bear upon the painting of portraits he manifested in the treatment of landscape, and by means of them attained similarly fine results. Once again he had to decide what selection to make out of the infinity of objects presented by nature, and again he determined by industry to depict as much and to omit as little as possible, and in selecting it was his aim to render the character of a scene in the same way that he endeavoured to render the character of a man. In the 'St. Francis' landscape, for example, he imitates with perfect veracity the bedding of a sandstone rock

T

and the wilderness all around is of fitting kind, as any one acquainted, for example, with Rustall Common near Tunbridge Wells may verify for himself. The only mistake is that the growth of flowers in the close grass is too luxuriant for a sandy soil, but the presence of the saint and the miraculous vision overhead may surely be excuse enough for that. The flowers themselves would please a botanist as well as the stratified rock would satisfy the student of geology. Jan van Eyck knew no more science than Turner, but both of them had eyes to see and hands to fashion with, and in their ignorance they created what more learned men could not, with all their knowledge, have built so truly together.

The delight of Jan van Eyck's art to his contemporary artists must have been that its fundamental principles were patent, and such as all could adopt without delay. Patience, perseverance, an eye careful to observe, a memory trained to retain—that was all. So the artists of Flanders and Brabant set themselves with all speed to follow in the path of their great leader. Gold backgrounds were henceforward abjured, except by some old-fashioned and now forgotten painters, and every one began to open his eyes to the world of nature. It was an auspicious hour. A new epoch was about to dawn, creation was widening to the view of men. Curiously enough, however, the landscapes chosen for painting were never yet the flat lands, but always hilly country watered by a stately river, or at the least by a winding stream—country such as that along the valley of the Maas. The beauty of the flats and fens was one day to be learnt by the Dutch, but only after they had watered with their blood the soil they had wrung from the sea, and so made it dearer than a thousand countries of mountain and primeval forest.

In two of Roger van der Weyden's pictures, the Middelburg and St. Columba altar-pieces, the town of Brussels is introduced into the background. But landscape does not occupy an important position with Roger, and in this, as in other matters, his sympathy for the old Köln school comes visibly to the fore. In the case of at any rate one picture, his great ' Descent from the Cross,' he employed a gold background again, and many of the panels painted in his school are similarly adorned. It was a common custom with Roger's followers to copy single heads out of their master's large groups. Such single heads always have gold backgrounds, usually dotted over with little black dashes. Examples of school pictures of the kind may be seen in the National Gallery, the Brussels Museum, and elsewhere. Just as the strength of Jan van Eyck's portraiture faded somewhat under the hand of Roger, so it was with his landscape. But even as Memling (and the followers of Roger generally) gave a wider extension to the school of portraiture, so also did they enlarge the boundaries of the landscape art.

As landscape painters, the most prominent of Roger's followers were Dirck Bouts and Hans Memling. The former was an artist of power, whose pictures are always worth looking at.* He occupied the position of official painter to the municipality of Louvain, and his pictures were of a municipal as opposed to a courtly type. His models for prophets and saints are chosen from the craftsman class rather than from the nobility. His women are all honest house-wives and burgher maidens, dressed indeed in sumptuous garments, but wearing them in anything but a high-born style. Though all Bouts' pictures bear the traces of Roger van der Weyden's influence, they also prove that the painter had imbibed much of the spirit of Jan van Eyck. Bouts came nearer to Van Eyck than Roger did, or perhaps cared to do. The younger artist was a more thorough Fleming, more downright and straightforward than his Tournai-born master. Thus he not only bestowed upon nature a more intimate study, but he painted the faces of men with minuter accuracy. Still he

* There are two of them in the National Gallery, one a 'Madonna with Saints' ascribed to Hugo van der Goes, the other a dated portrait of the artist himself ascribed to Memling. The 'Exhumation of Saint Hubert' in the same gallery is not by Bouts.

was not so good an artist as Roger ; he had not the
swiftness of insight to seize gestures and expressions,

THE LAST SUPPER. BY DIRCK BOUTS. *Louvain.*

and his technical knowledge, as to perspective and
the like, contained many gaps.   He was a good
colourist, and where patience availed he was strong ;

where genius was essential he took a place in the second or even the third rank.

In many of Bouts' pictures the landscape is the main thing, and the figures are almost of the nature of accessories. The same cannot be said of the works of any earlier master, so that in this respect Bouts showed himself original. The wings of the 'Adoration of the Magi' at Munich, and the remarkable picture of newly-risen souls in the 'Garden of Paradise' (if that indeed be its subject) now at Lille, are good examples of Bouts' style as a landscape painter. The Lille picture is certainly founded on a study of the 'Adoration of the Lamb.' A hilly garden watered with the Fountain of Life and shadowed by scattered clumps of trees, fills the whole panel. It is peopled by companies of almost nude people, whom their gestures and expressions show to be under the influence of religious emotion. Each company is conducted by an angel to the Fountain of Life, and thence to the summit of a mountain (probably meant for the Mount of Olives), where falling down to adore they are carried up to heaven in turn and received within the sunset-tinted clouds.

It is remarkable that Bouts was the first to attempt the painting of sunset; Memling and several others followed him, but he led the way. We may imagine him at Louvain, after his day's work was done, wandering forth into the fields and watching with delight the golden orb sink behind the myriad-coloured tapestries of the west. The evening alone in these northern climes rendered him the harvest of rich tint which his colour-loving eye delighted in with the avidity of an Arab. What the painter loves to behold he sooner or later strives himself to create. Claude was not altogether the first "to set the sun in heaven." Bouts was before him by some two centuries, more or less. In the St. Christofer wing the full round orb of the westering sun stares you in the face from out of a sky barred with red stripes of cloud. The rocky precipices of the river-bank shut in the view on either hand; the rippled water leads past many a castle-crowned hill, like a highway paved with gold, to the golden portal of the sunset. The idea of the landscape might have been taken from the Rhine by the Lorlei rock, or possibly enough from some unrecognized scene in the Liège country. The transparencies, reflections, shadows, and ripple-forms of the water have been carefully studied from nature, and the rocky precipice on the left, if something exaggerated in steepness, is certainly founded upon a natural original, for no artist at that time could have invented so just a form for the stratification of the rock. The precipice on the other side is a good deal less natural; it is the kind of thing that might have come out of the painter's head. In order to fill the background with the unwonted aspect of full sunlight, the foreground is made darker than had ever before been done. It is only by a contrast with darkness that light can be shown. No man, much less a painter of Bouts' power, could have learnt at the first attempt how to treat correctly a subject so new and so difficult. Landscape art had to be practised by the Van de Veldes, Cuyps, Claudes, and Turners of the future before its expressional power could be complete. Bouts could not attain completeness, he could only feel after some expression, however inadequate, for the beauty which he saw daily fleeting before him, and which he would so gladly fix for ever upon a panel of his own.

The humble craftsman of Louvain, for humble every touch of his brush shows him to have been, is therefore memorable not so much for what he attained as for what he attempted and led others to attempt. He lengthened the scale of light and shade. He added evening to the daylight which alone had been attempted before him. And, in his choice of landscape, he enlarged the visible area of earth and sky brought into the background, and diminished in proportion the scale of his figures. He shows us as only Van Eyck had done, and he but seldom, wide stretches of country and vistas of valley. He heightened the canopy of his sky and widened its curtains, and so gave to nature more of the dignity which had previously been reserved for human or

THE ENTOMBMENT. BY DIRCK BOUTS. *National Gallery.*

saintly personages. Comparing the Archbishop of Köln's 'Madonna' with this St. Christofer, we get a measure of the change which a century had pro-duced. In the former the Virgin is colossal, the background is a curtain, and the foreground a green carpet of turf with an arabesque of flowers; in the latter, though the hero is a legendary giant, his figure is relatively small in a panel, nine tenths of which is occupied by river and rock, mountain and sky.

After Bouts landscape became more and more a subject of attention to artists. Memling, who seems likewise to have been a pupil of Roger van der Weyden, added to the traditions of the art of Bruges the same element that Bouts had made popular at Louvain. His peculiar disposition "half helped, half hindered him." He loved fairy tales, and could only paint with success pictures the subject of which was of the fairy kind, or could be treated in that spirit. Thus the only landscape that he could paint success-fully was the landscape of his own fairy-land, where it is always day, always fine weather, always spring-time, always warm, and always calm. No stormy skies, no rocky precipices, no raging seas, no flaring sunsets could he depict. Now and again he had to paint a sunset; if so he put it away in the corner of a large picture, and filled all the rest of the sky with the tender afternoon glow of a summer's day, which he loved best. He could not bring himself to throw the foreground into shadow as Bouts had done. All his foregrounds are lit in the same manner, and were probably painted first, the background being afterwards added, and if a sunset was necessary, why it had to be painted in. Some of the prettiest pieces of Memling's landscape are to be found ·in the background of the Munich picture of the ' Light of the World.' That picture includes a multitude of incidents occurring at all hours of the day and night—the Magi beholding the star, the angel appearing by night to the shepherds, the Resurrection early in the morning, and the Ascension at the moment of sunset. The sunset in this case is painted in one corner, the edge of the departing orb being red on the western horizon of still lagoon. All the rest of the picture is in full daylight, and the star is only brought into prominence by the use of·gold. The wide landscape, like the rest of the picture, must not be regarded as one whole, but as a group of little landscapes arbitrarily joined together for a certain end. The structure of mountains and rocks is not so good as with Van Eyck or Bouts. Memling usually makes the stratification of his rocks lie vertically. He thus fills his picture with a quantity of mounds of ugly form, their sides being steep and their caps of monotonously uniform shape. The charm of his landscapes must be sought in other kinds of subject. It is in country roads wind·ng

amongst fields, in slowly meandering brooks, in little
bridges and water-mills, in cottages by the wayside,
in flowery meadows, tranquil bays, verdant shores,
and pleasant copses that he finds his joy and richly
shares it with whoever will look. Details of flower
and plant he paints as well as his predecessors, but
his special province is the widening distance, where
the atmosphere comes into play as a colouring power.
He shares with Bouts the power of carrying the fancy
far away into the blue, and shedding upon what is
distant such a charm as that wherewith memory
invests the past and hope the future.

Before and even after Memling's day it was customary to hand over the outsides of a picture's wings
for a pupil to paint with monochrome figures in
imitation of wood-sculptures. One of the best of
Memling's pictures, however,—the little 'Adoration
of the Magi' triptych at Bruges,—has, on the outsides
of its wings, two charming figures of saints, seated
in the foreground of a lovely landscape. No better
example could be quoted to show how, towards the
close of the fifteenth century, landscape art was
gaining in popularity. It had ousted the gold background ; now it relegated sculpture to canopies and
frames. The landscape background in question is,
moreover, one of the best Memling ever painted.
Generally speaking, his rock-structure is a weak
point, but here he has evidently had some definite

scene before him as a model. It is a river view, and
does duty for the Jordan, where John is in the act of
pouring water over the head of Christ, whilst an angel
stands by, holding his Master's robes. The river fills
the bottom of a valley, lying between steep and
rounded hills, the slopes of which have been cut and
worn away below by the flowing stream, so that they
rise vertically out of the water, and only begin to
round themselves over when a point is reached where
the water action ceases. The form of the hills is just
what it would be in nature, and whilst no geologist
could desire a truer delineation, the artistic treatment
of line and colour satisfies every æsthetic requirement.

During the whole of the fifteenth century the art
of miniature and illumination was much practised at
Bruges. The miniaturists had their own peculiar
method ; they always painted upon parchment in
what were called "lime colours." In the first half
of the century they were not organized into a guild ;
nevertheless it was legally decided by the magistrates
of the town, in giving judgment on an important
case, that no miniaturist might trespass upon the
domain of the painters' guild, and no painter might
make miniatures for sale. A miniaturist might only
paint in lime colours on parchment ; he might not
employ oil colours, neither might he paint on panel.
The nearest approach to an ordinary picture per-

mitted to him was a painting upon parchment glued on to panel, and of pictures done in that way a few survive.* About the year 1457 the booksellers, printers, binders, scribes, miniaturists, and others whose business was the making of books of one kind and another, associated themselves into a religious confraternity under the patronage of St. John the Evangelist. They agreed upon rules to regulate the exercise of their trade, and, in June 1457 (Beffroi, iv. 238), they obtained a confirmation from the municipality, and thenceforward took their place amongst the recognized guilds of the town. From this time onward no one could work as a painter of miniatures, within the *commune* of Bruges, unless he were a member of the guild of St. John the Evangelist. At the end of the fifteenth century we find a few artists belonging both to the painters' and miniaturists' guilds, Gerard David being the most notable instance ; but, as a rule, the two crafts were kept entirely distinct.

The history of miniature painting in Flanders is thus independent of the history of oil painting. Of course the two arts acted and reacted upon one another, though not to the extent we might have expected. Types of figures are the same, and the feeling for character is similarly strongly expressed

---

* One by Gerard David's wife belonging to Mr. Willett, and one by G. David in the Camarin di S. Theresa at the Escurial.

in both arts, but the miniaturists had independent
traditions of their own. To trace the growth and
development of these traditions would be a work of
time ; the most rapid glance over the whole field must
here suffice. In the Gothic age France was the centre
of the best miniature painting, and French influence
was everywhere predominant. Other countries had
their local schools, but none of them were altogether
independent. By degrees, how-
ever, the local schools grew
stronger, and the French influence became matter of history only. Such a local school
sprang up in the Lower Rhine
country, with Köln for its
centre, and during the fourteenth century miniatures of
the Köln type were painted

FROM THE "HOURS" OF THE
DUC DE BERRI. *Paris.*

in many parts of Flanders.
But when the Low Countries
passed under the rule of the Dukes of Burgundy, and
the great epoch of independent Flemish art commenced, miniature painting manifested a new and
sudden vigour, just as Flemish oil painting did. The
direct patronage of the Court did much to foster the
rising art. Duke Philip the Good, to whom Flemish
culture owed so much, was an ardent lover of beautiful books. He was eager to form a library of magnifi-

cently written, illuminated, and bound volumes, and for this purpose he maintained a great proportion of the best workmen continually in his employ. His example was imitated by the nobles of his court and the wealthy men of the kingdom in general. Not only were sumptuous books of devotion required in great numbers, but huge editions of chronicles, romances, poems, and other secular works were ordered, and it became customary to illustrate them with a quantity of beautifully painted miniatures, either in mono- chrome or in colours. Of such volumes the consider- able remnant of the Burgundian Library, now pre- served in the Brussels Museum, contains many noble examples, and it is only by inspecting them at first hand that an idea of the multitude and excellence of the works of fifteenth-century Flemish and Brabant- ine miniaturists can be attained.

In an illuminated volume there are two pictorial elements which can be considered apart, the orna- mental borders to the pages, and the actual minia- tures. The miniatures, from the very nature of the case, had to be treated with more originality than oil paintings demanded. They had to represent all manner of subjects, and though the editor of the volume usually gave tolerably minute directions as to the composition of each subject, the artist was left much more to his own devices in the matter than a painter could be in the treatment of one of the round

U

of religious subjects upon which painters had been engaged for some hundred of years. It was the miniaturists who had to learn how to depict a battle, or the burning of a town, or any of the hundred incidents upon which chroniclers and romance writers of the time loved to dwell. Naturally, therefore, miniature painters were early attracted towards landscape, and indeed there were other forces urging them in the same direction. In former days manuscript illumination had been the work of monks, and the monastery had usually been well able to afford the gold and silver which the elaborate and gorgeous Gothic backgrounds required. But when the public began to ask for beautiful books of devotion, whatever could be done in the way of diminishing expense by the artist, now a layman and dependent upon his craft for his daily bread, brought his productions within the reach of a larger number of buyers. For this reason diapered backgrounds, and finally plain gold backgrounds, had to give way, and landscape and sky of necessity took their place. Economical circumstances combined with the development of the national ideal towards the same result. The growing love of nature found a place prepared by circumstances for its satisfaction.

The borders show an even more marked progress in the same direction. Gothic illuminators loved to adorn capital letters with long and beautiful flourishes

extending all about the margin of the page, in which
foliation was mingled with little birds, beasts, and
grotesque figures, or the tail of the letter itself might
be fashioned into the form of some fantastic creature.
As long as the spirit of fantasy reigned supreme,
nothing is more charming than its productions of this
kind. But, by degrees, a change took place. The
naïve little creatures become more and more natural,
and are combined to express incidents of folk life
sometimes of an unpleasantly gross character. This
treatment involved the loss of the free and decorative
character which had been the charm of the early
work, and soon the borders became bounded by hard
and fast oblong outlines, within which little pictures
of the ordinary kind might have been included.
That, however, was contrary to the idea of a border,
the intention of which was merely decorative. The
old foliation, therefore, confined within fixed limits,
developed into something new. The borders became
the home of flowers, and‘the miniaturists of Bruges
adopted the fashion with enthusiasm. Flowers have
for centuries possessed special attractions for the
people of the Low Countries. You can hardly find
a Flemish painting of the fifteenth century in which
they do not play an important part. They had their
symbolic meanings, and were chosen with definite intention to enforce the moral of the picture. In Hugo
van der Goes' 'Nativity,' painted for a Florentine

U 2

patron, there is a pot of flowers in the foreground—
the lily for the Virgin, the columbine for the Holy
Ghost, and the iris for the badge of Florence. Cut
flowers were the choice of the illuminators. They
painted them in their borders just as they lay fresh
upon the painter's table. And they painted them
with all a miniaturist's care and love of detail; they
hurried over nothing, but gave them the modelling,
the textures, and the colours of nature as far as their
skill permitted.

During the last half of the fifteenth century, when
the art of Flemish miniature culminated, printing
and wood-engraving advanced with rapid strides.
They were destined to destroy the illuminator's art,
but before destroying it they helped it to its perfection. Printed books at once supplanted in the
market all except the best kind of manuscripts.
An illuminator was obliged to work with great
fineness and skill in order to satisfy employers,
rendered more than ever fastidious by the beautiful productions of the printing press. A roughly-
painted wood-cut was as good as a poorly done
miniature, and could be made at a less cost. Already
before 1490 the noble author Olivier de la Marche
had committed a poem to the hands of a Gouda
printer, and though the wood-cuts in the printed
book were afterwards carefully coloured, in the
case of a few copies, the amount of work given

APRIL. *From the Grimani Breviary.*

to miniaturists was much less than that taken away from them. The Bruges guild of illuminators were thus forced to produce work of high excellence in order to retain a market for their services. For some years they remained equal to the demands made upon them. The guild seems to have undertaken large pieces of work and then to have divided each amongst its members. Thus the finest volume illuminated and written in the last half of the fifteenth century was thus made, the famous Grimani Breviary now in the Doge's Palace at Venice. The leading artists of the Bruges guild co-operated to produce it. Some undertook the writing, others certain borders, others divided the miniatures between them, and eventually the pages were collected and bound together into a single volume. By such co-operation the work was more rapidly advanced, and a pleasing variety was attained in lieu of the monotonous repetition of a single man's handiwork. The Grimani Breviary has long been deservedly famous, and, in the old days of promiscuous attribution, it used to be said that many of the pages were the work of Memling himself. Modern investigation, however, has shown that this could not be, because Memling, not being a member of the guild of St. John, was precluded from trespassing upon the monopoly of the miniaturist. The pages assigned to him were done by Gerard David and his wife. The Grimani

Breviary stands alone in point of size and elaboration, but other manuscripts have been recognized
as coming from the same source; such are a
beautiful little volume in the Court Library at
Vienna, another at Cassel, another belonging to the
Rothschilds, and some half-dozen elsewhere known
to Mr. Weale.

The best of the Bruges miniaturists at the end of
the fifteenth century was certainly Gerard David.
But he was even more remarkable as an oil painter.
Up till quite recently all his pictures were assigned to
Memling, but the labours of Mr. Weale have given
him a renewed individuality. We now know the
best of his pictures, and find that we even possess a
portrait of him from his own hand. His most finished
works are two altar-pieces, one in the Museum at
Rouen, the other, representing the ' Baptism of Christ,'
in the Academy at Bruges. In the history of landscape painting the Baptism triptych is important. The
subject had long been a favourite with artists, but never
before had the landscape been made so important a
feature in the composition. One of Roger van der
Weyden's panels at Berlin may be taken as an
example of the earlier method of treatment. There
the landscape is merely an accessory, handled with
care indeed, but not finished with the same minuteness
as the faces and figures. With Roger the sentiment
of the event is supreme. But, by the end of the

THE MADONNA AND SAINTS. BY GERARD DAVID. *Rouen.*

To face p. 296.

fifteenth century, religious sentiment had become
weak. So David painted Christ, the Baptist, and the
angel in a perfunctory manner, but devoted himself
with zeal to the elaboration of surrounding natural
objects. He must have made many careful studies
from nature before he could undertake such a landscape. Compare for example the rippled water here
with that in Roger's 'Madonna with St. Luke,' or Bouts'
'St. Christofer.' Roger's ripples (if indeed the picture
be by Roger) are little more than symbols. Bouts
shows a considerable advance, and in some individual
wavelets leaves little to be desired, but he combines
them together with too much regularity. David's
work is evidently the result of many days of careful
observation. He has caused a man to wade into an
actual pond, and watched the concentric circles ex-
panding around his legs, the two systems intersecting
one another and passing on undisturbed to the river-
bank. He has made advances too in representing
transparencies of water, and he has not neglected
either the reflections or the shadows upon the surface.
Comparing the water here with that in which St.
Christofer stands in Memling's altar-piece (hanging
together in the same room at Bruges), the advance
effected by David cannot be gainsaid. Memling's
figures are finer, his picture enshrines a more excellent
religious sentiment, but his landscape cannot be
measured against David's.

Nor was it merely in the representation of water that David advanced ; he brought together a larger number of natural objects naturally combined. His sky is more varied with clouds, his trees are of many different kinds, and are studied individually from nature. His landscape has a wider spread and includes scenery of different characters. He has studied the banks of streams as well as the surface of the flowing waters, and he knows what plants grow in the shallows, or clamber over the edges of the grass. Moreover, he was, I believe, the first painter to think of the shadow-giving nature of trees. Trees had for many years formed a favourite subject for backgrounds, but even by Memling they were rather conventionally rendered, one by one, not grouped into woods, and seldom brought into the foreground. In David's ' Baptism,' and again in the wing of a diptych in the National Gallery, we have a wood brought near us, with its domed canopy of foliage above, and its labyrinth of trunks buried in sylvan twilight below. In such a gloom John Baptist stands with his disciples when Christ passes by. The foliage too is painted with more knowledge of the differences between one tree and another. In some, great boughs thrust out their muscular arms as though each was the bearer of an ægis, in others the branches are lightly tufted with a young green spray.

Here and there David's landscapes show traces

of a tendency towards a fantastic treatment of the scene. Mountains now and again threaten to over-hang, or jut their sides into the air with an unusual precipitancy. This exaggeration of natural forms is however rare, the artist being still unwilling to attract the beholder's attention away from the figures which tell the tale the picture was painted to enshrine.

Joachim de Patenier (died 1524), whom Dürer visited and entitled the "good landscape painter," felt none of the restraints which, it must be admitted, operated well upon David. One of his best pictures is likewise a 'Baptism of Christ,'* and has also a 'Preaching of John' in the background. If David's landscape is wide, Patenier's is much wider. It embraces miles of country and opens on.every side. The rippling water and clustering herbage are not painted in the same minute detail, a broader handling being substituted in the foreground, for which the artist felt less attraction than for the distance. Some far-away cottage by the river-side, some hamlet nestling against a remote hill-slope, some castle on a craggy peak, blue against the transparent sky—· such objects were a joy to him, he loved to ponder over every detail in them. Moreover, with Patenier the fantastic element was of much importance. He wished his landscapes to be romantic, to contain

* In the Belvedere, phot. Miethke and Wawra.

qualities not ordinarily seen in the landscape even
of the Maas valley, where his own birthplace lay,
still less in the neighbourhood of Bruges. He would
have precipitous rocks rising like obelisks out of
water or plain.   He would build them up into
fantastic forms, like the seracs of an ice-fall, and
would perch little huts upon inaccessible ledges, or
hollow out caves to be the hiding-places of strange
beasts.   His rivers must pass through gorges or
under natural archways ; his skies must be full of
moving clouds ; his wide districts of country must
present contrasts of rocky mountain walls and fertile
plains.   From Van Eyck downwards, the homely
scenery of undulating country had found its way into
pictures.   Plenty of slow winding streams, wooded
meadows, water-mills, and (in miniatures) corn-fields
and plough-lands had been depicted.   But Patenier's
eye wandered over a wider area ; he saw the village
with its wind-mill and its fields, the hill-side where
the flocks grazed in the sunlight, the broad river
with its ferry-boats, the cart-road, the mule-track,
and the bridge leading to the toll-gate.   He saw
also the grandeur of wild scenery, and strove,
though not with perfect success, to bring that into
his pictures, showing thereby the possession of a
foretaste of that delight in nature for her own sake
the full enjoyment of which has been reserved for
the people of our own century.

Patenier's love of the wild and the fantastic
enabled him to paint certain subjects, such as the
legend of St. Christofer, better than any of his predecessors had done. Property to depict the legendary
scene involved, as has been said, the representation
of a river rushing along in flood, with a giant hard
put to it to struggle across it by his wonted ford.
Such painters as Memling never attempted to give
an idea of the force of the swollen stream, but satisfied themselves with drawing a mere symbolic ditch.
Even Bouts was content when he had covered the
rock-bound river with a crisp surface of little ripples.
Patenier for the first time (in a picture at Madrid *)
rendered the force of a river in flood, its waters
spread abroad over miles of country, inundating
village, field, and town, and bearing forward their
burden of drowned humanity.

Patenier's example was infectious, as any student
of early sixteenth-century Flemish art will soon
discover. For several decades landscape supplanted
figures in the estimation of many stay-at-home artists.
The men who went to Italy and fell under the sway
of Raphael and Michelangelo wasted their lives in
attempting to work in a style for which by birth and
education they were unsuited. Those who stayed at
home were more and more driven to that kind of
work for which nature intended them—the painting

* Phot. Braun.

of their home-scenery and home-life. But they had to wait for more than a century before a great painter arose to ennoble the art which, in their own heart of hearts, they all loved best. And then they turned away from Madonnas and Saints to the cows of the pasture, the pigs of the farmyard, and the horses of the fair; from the landscape of heaven with its population of the blest to the flats of Holland and the boers of the tavern and the skittle-ground; from the angelic hierarchies of the firmament to the ships of the sea and the fishing-boats of Scheveningen.

The change was finally accomplished in the heat of Revolution and the turmoil of triumphant Protestantism, and not till it was accomplished did men learn the lesson, that the power of art is independent of creeds, dogmas, and philosophies, and rests alone upon the exhaustless capacity of men for delight in the world of nature and the realms of fancy.

CHAPTER IX.

TAPESTRIES.*

WIIEN any art reaches a period of culmination, it always carries others with it to a high pitch of development. Thus when architecture culminated in the thirteenth century, all the decorative arts that could contribute to its glory were likewise encouraged and increased by its power and success. The fifteenth century in the Low Countries was again the day of an art maximum. Painting was the leading art, but it did not stand alone. The arts of the goldsmith, the engraver, the builder, the miniaturist, the furniture

---

* The materials for this chapter have been chiefly derived · from the following works :—

J. J. Guiffrey, *Hist. de la T.*, Paris, 1878, etc., fol.

E. Muntz, *La Tap.*, Paris, 1883, 8vo—a very useful popular work.

Darcel, Paris, s. d., fol.

Deville, *Dict. Tap.*, Paris, 1878-80, 4to.

M. L. A. Jubinal, *Anc. Tap. historiées*, Paris, 1838, obl. fol.

Arch. hist. et litt. du nord de la France et du midi de la Belg. 3ᵉ ser. t. vi. p. 170 (*Les hauts-lisseurs d'Arras et de Lille*).

maker, and many others were cultivated with success,
and the art of tapestry-weaving reached a degree
of perfection never since attained. This statement
will probably not command universal assent, because,
in the opinion of many, finer productions were turned
out by the looms of other countries, especially of
France, at a later date. Whether the forms depicted
and the colours combined in French tapestry are
really charming or not is doubtless a matter of
taste; but tapestry, like all other arts, has its laws
of right and wrong, deducible from the nature of
the materials employed, and the method of their
employment, and any one who will investigate these,
and then compare the fifteenth-century Flemish
tapestries with the later products of the looms of
France, will find that Arras is far in advance of
Gobelins in obedience to fundamental laws.

The earliest hangings made in Northern Europe
in the Christian era were embroideries, and the most
famous existing specimens of such work are the
so-called Bayeaux tapestries, which are not really
tapestries at all. In these and similar hangings the
subjects were embroidered with greater or less elaboration upon a plain piece of woven stuff. The work
was done by high-born ladies and their maidens
within castle bowers, or by nuns in their convents.
Few remnants of such hangings remain, but the
multitude of them that must once have existed may

be deduced from the romances and songs of those
ancient days.

Stuffs adorned with woven patterns were then
usually imported from the sunny East. Fine dresses,
state robes, wall hangings, and rich draperies of all
sorts were made of Oriental goods. At Vienna, for
example, the traveller may still see the imperial robes
of the Holy Roman Emperor. He will find the border
of the coronation garments of the supreme head
of Christendom embroidered with verses from the
Koran. Indeed so accustomed did Europeans become
to such embroidered hems of Arabic inscriptions,
that even when they made fine stuffs for themselves,
they adorned their edges with a hem of letters forming
no readable words, but merely put together to imitate
the to them illegible Arabic texts. Such borders are
continually seen on the draperies of the Christ, the
Virgin, and saints in paintings of the Flemish school,
whilst there are three pictures in the Berlin Museum *
in which the very halo of the Mother of God is adorned
with imitation Arabic letters, which if they mean
anything stand for a quotation from the words of
Mahomet.

When the weaving of fine stuffs came to be a
staple industry of the Low Countries it was divided
into two classes of work. There were the making of
tapestries, properly so called, that is to say, of woven

* Squarcione (27 A), Mantegna (27), Borgognone (51).

X

pictures, and the making of fine stuffs for garments, furniture embellishment, carpets, and other the like purely decorative purposes. The latter class of work was called Saracenic, because all such stuffs were made in imitation of imported Oriental originals. With it we need not further concern ourselves here.

Figured tapestry might be made in looms of two kinds, known respectively as high warp and low warp looms.* All the larger and more important tapestries were worked in high warp looms, and workers in that kind were the leaders of their craft. Low warp weavers turned out carpets and decorative stuffs oftener than figured tapestries.

Every art is a glorified handicraft. Every art in its waxing rises out of a handicraft, and in its decay sinks back into a handicraft again. The art of tapestry arose out of the handicraft of weaving. The Low Countries were the centre of weaving manu- facture in the Middle Ages. Their early municipal and industrial development, and their proximity to the chief wool-producing country, England, enabled them to attain command of the wool industry Flanders and Brabant grew rich by their weaving and their trade. Commerce brought fine examples of woven stuffs under their eyes, wealth created a demand for such stuffs, and an industry already in

* As to the technical process of tapestry making in these two kinds of looms, see the South Kensington handbook on Tapestry.

existence was ready to undertake the supply of the thing demanded. Thus every year the looms of Flanders turned out finer stuffs, and every year they attempted to surpass the productions of the preceding months.

The wealth and splendour of the Burgundian court was an encouragement and a support to the luxurious art. It is only necessary to look at the pictures of Van Eyck, Roger, Memling, and their fellows, in which the Virgin and saints wear the court costumes of the day, to see what a demand must at that time have existed for splendid stuffs, and how the crafts-men availed to satisfy it. Note, for instance, the robes of the King of Heaven in the 'Adoration of the Lamb' with their jewelled borders, the hangings of embroidered gold behind the throne, the rich vest-ments of the singing angels ; these alone would suffice to show the tendency of the art industries of the day.

Before storied hangings were woven in the work-shops of Flanders they were embroidered, as we have seen, in princely and baronial castles. The art thus from the earliest date received a secular impress, and this is the most important point for the student of art history to bear in mind. In the age of what we may call castle-power, the central Gothic epoch, most arts were chiefly employed in the service of the Church, and thus received a strong religious impress.

X 2

A few hunting-horns may be found carved with
images of the chase, a few ivory caskets adorned with
sculptured incidents from the poems of the Minne-
singers, but an overwhelming majority of the works
of mediæval art that have come down to us represent
religious subjects. Tapestry forms an exception to
this law. It was the nursery of secular art. The
Bayeaux hangings deal with incidents of war, and
such no doubt were the kind of subjects which the
knights loved to see embroidered in their halls.
When the scene of the industry was transferred from
the bower to the workshop, and the method of it was
changed from embroidery to a kind of weaving, the
subjects chosen for representation were not changed.
Prescription had already fixed them. A list of some
of the principal Flemish tapestries recorded in the
inventories of the possessions of princes and nobles
of that time will show this to be the case.

1384. Story of Froiment of Bordiaux.

1384. Story of William of Orange.

1386. Two persons throwing flowers in a wood.

1386. Story of Alexander and of Robert le
Fuselier.

1387. Story of Doon de la Roche.

1387. Shepherds and Shepherdesses.

1387. The battle of Rosebecque (in which Philip
van Artevelde was overthrown), a large and very
famous piece.

1393. Shepherds and Shepherdesses.
1394. The King of France and the Twelve Peers.
All the above were woven at Arras.

Duke Philip le Hardi, in 1404, possessed the following amongst other tapestries : — Semiramis, *l'Arc de Bergherie*, Guil. de Bomercy, *Rommant de la Rose*, Battle of Pont-Velain, Guy of Burgundy, Judas Maccabeus, King Arthur, Hector of Troy, Harpin of Bourges, Florence of Rome, Percival of Gaul, Lady between two lovers, Portraits of Madame d'Artois and Monseigneur de Flandres, *Dieu d'Amours dit des Bergiers*, and *Chastel de Franchise.*

In or about the year 1400 the Duke of Burgundy bought tapestries depicting the Story of Jason, the Story of Troy, the Story of Charles the Great, a Battle, and the Twelve Peers of France. In 1420 he bought a ' Fame ' and ' Lorens Guerin hunting the wild boar.' In 1449 he bought the Golden Fleece tapestries, which will demand attention later on.

Louis of Luxemburg in 1480 left fourteen pieces of tapestry representing the romance of Melusine, four representing the history of Julius Cæsar, and one of the *Trionfe des Dames.*

A few religious subjects are inventoried in the court lists, but the large majority are of the same kind as those above mentioned.

Besides such figured tapestries for chambers and halls, a sumptuously-furnished palace required other

decorative stuffs for the adornment of seats and
thrones. These stuffs were often woven to harmonize
with the wall tapestries, the whole forming one set
together. Louis of Luxemburg in 1480 had two
such rooms of state, in one of which the walls were
hung with four incidents from the romance of Godfrey
of Boulogne, and there were a dais, a curtain (for the
back of the throne), and a bed-cover to match. The
other room was hung with the 'Castle of Love', and
had a dais and curtain besides.

Most tapestry was thus woven for the palace, but
no inconsiderable amount was also employed in
churches. Sometimes indeed a noble would bequeath
his pieces of the Story of Jason or the Castle of Love
to a church, and they would be accepted and
willingly hung in some part of the sacred edifice·
As a rule, of course, tapestry woven for a church
dealt with religious subjects, and probably few if
any of the cathedrals of the fourteenth and fifteenth
centuries were without at any rate some woven
hangings. Indeed, in the fourteenth century a
certain need arose in cathedrals which tapestry was
best suited to supply.

When the bulk of the cathedrals were built, they
were built in consequence of a great popular movement, the bishops and the townsfolk being then, in
the main, allies having common interests, and working enthusiastically together towards common aims.

The fact of the cathedral-building movement was not the only sign of this alliance ; the plan and arrangement of the buildings themselves was partly determined by it. The orderliness and ceremonial of worship required certain divisions of the building during the times of service, but otherwise the whole interior of the church was accessible to the public and they might wander where they pleased in it. In the fourteenth century a change took place in this respect. The clergy were' increased in number and wealth, and they no longer felt the same need of popular support as before. Cathedral services became less popular ; they took more and more the form of ecclesiastical ceremonies only concerning the clerical body. The folk, left more and more to themselves, became less and less reverent, and their festivals had soon to be banished into the streets and market-places. Then it was that nave and choir were separated from one another by a stone screen, the choir being surrounded by some low wall, above which, from pillar to pillar, it was usual to hang tapestries, thus making the choir practically a closed chapel into which the folk could not even look.

In the year 1402 the master-weaver, Pierre Féré, of Arras was employed to make a set of tapestries illustrative of the Legend of St. Piat, which were intended to close the choir of Tournai Cathedral in this fashion. Some of them may be seen at Tournai

to the present day. At Reims, Beauvais, and elsewhere similar tapestries can likewise be found in
which the subjects represented are religious.

A certain group of churches exists in France, the
most famous of them being the church of St. Maurice
of Angers, governed in their design by the intention
that tapestry should form their chief internal decoration. Large spaces of wall were left blank in them
where tapestries were permanently to hang. The
Angers tapestries together measured one hundred
and sixty metres long by five feet deep. They used
to hang all round the nave and choir of the church
above the great arcade. Each piece was in two rows
of seven compositions representing incidents from the
Apocalypse. A border ran all along the top depicting Heaven ; a corresponding border at the bottom
represented the Earth.*

These, the most famous existing church tapestries,
were likewise woven in the high warp looms of
Flanders between the years 1380 and 1495. The
pictures were founded on the miniatures in a still
existing manuscript † which at that time belonged to
King Charles I. of France, and was lent by him for
the purpose to the Duke of Anjou, the donor of the

* See L. de Joannis, *Les Tapisseries de la Cath. d'Angers*,
Angers, 1864, fol. B. de Montault, *Not. Archéol. sur les Tap.
de la Cath. d'A.*, Angers, 1875, 8vo. *L'Art.* vii. (1876), p. 300.
† Bibliothèque Nationale, Paris, *fonds français*, r.o. 403.

tapestries. Looking at the tapestries themselves, it is easy to see that their designs come from the fourteenth century. The figures are all of Gothic type, but with the graceful bending forms and flowing drapery outlines such as we find in work of early Köln artists and their contemporaries. There is something too of the sweetness of sentiment which pervaded the pictorial art of the day, as, for instance, in the pretty angels where they walk over the sea of glass singing the song of the Lamb. St. John is always standing by, looking on, and his face shows several varieties of expression. His hair stands on end at times with naïve literalness. The backgrounds are always filled with foliation finely treated as a decorative arabesque. One compartment shows the Lamb standing upon Mount Zion, and the beholder is inclined to ask whether Van Eyck may not have had the cartoon for this tapestry in mind when designing his picture of the 'Adoration of the Lamb.'

The church of Douai was likewise rich in Flemish tapestries of the best period dealing with religious subjects. Such were six pieces of the Deadly Sins, nine pieces of the Story of the Three Kings, two of the Story of Jacob, one of the Queen of Sheba, and one of Christ's agony in the Garden.

Tapestries, again, formed convenient princely presents, and the Dukes of Burgundy were notably

generous in this fashion.   Thus, in 1423 the Duke
paid a heavy price to the Bruges merchant, Giovanni
Arnolfini of Lucca, the same whose portrait by Jan
van Eyck adorns the National Gallery, for six
tapestries of Our Lady's life to be sent as a
present to the Pope.   Duke Philip le Hardi too gave
several tapestries to Richard the Second's uncles, the
Dukes of Gloucester and Lancaster, when they came
as ambassadors to negotiate a peace with the uncles
of the King of France.   On that same occasion, the
old chronicler tells us, the ambassadors "chose for
meeting-place a thatched chapel of poor appearance
near the ruined village of Lelingen between Calais
and Boulogne.   Spacious pavilions were erected in
the neighbouring plain in the form of a camp, and
they were hung about within with tapestries of wool
and rich silk stuffs charming to the eye.   The tent
of the Duke of Burgundy was of specially great size,
such as had never been seen before.   The structure
was so rich and elegant that it delighted every one.
. . . To hide the aged condition of the chapel walls
the Duc de Berri had caused woollen tapestries to be
hung all around, representing divers ancient battles.
But after the first interview the Duke of Lancaster
had them removed, saying that men seeking for
peace should not have pictures of combats and the
destruction of towns before their eyes.   So these
tapestries were replaced by other gold embroideries

representing the chief incidentsin the Passion of our Lord Jesus, and the Duke much approved of the change."

Such passages not only afford circumstantial evidence of the multitude of tapestries which must then have existed, but show the varied uses to which they were put. When a prince was to make a state entry into a town, or when there was to be any great civic festival or procession, a crier went round beforehand and invited the inhabitants to make the finest display they could. Then all the house fronts were hung with tapestries, or at least with painted sheets in imitation of them, such as those which Hugo van der Goes made with rapid skill. Or, again, in whatever house a prince was to lodge for the night on a journey, the chambers were if possible hung with tapestries, either carried from place to place in the prince's train or collected from all the country round. Thus upon the occasion of a journey of Charles V. through the Netherlands, the Regent Mary of Hungary gave orders that the country gentry should lend their tapestry to decorate the chambers at Valenciennes where the Emperor was to spend a night or two. The collection was to be made at the Government's expense, and it was guaranteed that the tapestries should be returned uninjured. In earlier times the wealthy Duke of Burgundy carried even his finest tapestries about with him. When

Louis XI. entered Paris after his coronation, Jacques du Clercq relates that "the Duke of Burgundy caused the hall and chambers of his Hôtel d'Artois to be hung with the finest tapestry that had ever been seen in Paris, especially that of the History of Gideon. He had also the History of Alexander, and many more, all made of gold and silver and silk, and because they were so many he had them hung one over another."

The tapestries of the History of Gideon, thus once again referred to, were the most famous turned out of the looms of the Low Countries when the art had attained perfect development. The contract for them was entered into in 1449 between Duke Philip the Good and Robert Dury and Jean de l'Ortie, master tapestry weavers of Tournai. It was bargained that the cartoons should be designed by Bauduin de Bailleul, artist designer of Arras, or by a better if such could be found. "What is yellow in the cartoons shall be of fine gold Venetian thread, and what is white shall be of fine silver Venetian thread, save and except the faces and flesh parts, . . . and the rest of the tapestry shall be of good and fine silks, . . . of the best colours that can be found." Eventually the Duke also bought in the cartoons for a round sum of money. The tapestries were finished in the year 1453, and not in 1456, as the following passage from Chastellain seems to suggest. Writing of the seventeenth chapter of the Order of the Golden Fleece, which was held at the Hague in 1456, he tells how "the Hall at the Hague is one of the finest in the world, and best suited for great festivals. There was there hung some of the richest tapestry that ever belonged to a king, and of the largest size. It had never been shown before, for it had just been newly made for the Duke, its subject being the miracle of the Fleece in the story of Gideon, which the Duke appropriated to his order."

At Paris, on the occasion of Louis XI.'s coronation, it made, as we have seen, an equal sensation. Jacques du Clercq speaks of it as "the noblest tapestry ever seen in France, which the Duke had had made all of gold and silk for love of the Order of the Fleece which he bore, which fleece Gideon prayed our Lord should be made wet and then dry, as in the Bible *on le peut plus aisément veoir*. And this he had taken for the badge of his order, not wishing to take the Fleece which Jason won in the Isle of Colchis, because Jason broke his faith."

The after-history of these tapestries can be followed with tolerable continuity. They were used on the occasion of the marriage of Charles the Bold in 1468. In 1498 they adorned the church at Brussels for a royal baptism. They figured in 1555 at the ceremony of Charles the Fifth's abdication. Ten years later they adorned the wedding of Alexander Farnese.

They were probably carried to Vienna in 1794, with the rest of the property of the Order of the Golden Fleece. The present writer believes that he saw one of them hung amidst a quantity of old tapestry in the Court Church at Vienna on the occasion of the marriage of the present Crown Prince of Austria.

The town of Arras was of course the centre of the industry at the time of its highest development. The art was indeed introduced into Paris as early as 1302, but it did not become a great art there. It must have reached Arras about 1350, though it is not definitely mentioned till 1367, when tapestry weaving is spoken of as a flourishing industry. The municipal authorities did all they could to foster it, and the weavers rapidly increased in number and wealth. The best period of the art at Arras was the first half of the fifteenth century; after the turn of the century it began to decline. In the seventeen years preceding 1450 forty-six new names were entered in the books of the guild; in the next seventeen years only thirteen were added. Louis XI. when he captured Arras (4th May, 1477) struck the death-blow to the industry. The population of the town hated their new master, so in 1479 he ordered the whole lot of them to be summarily expelled, the town to be renamed, and a new population collected to inhabit it. The new population, however, could not weave, and so the town sank, as any one might

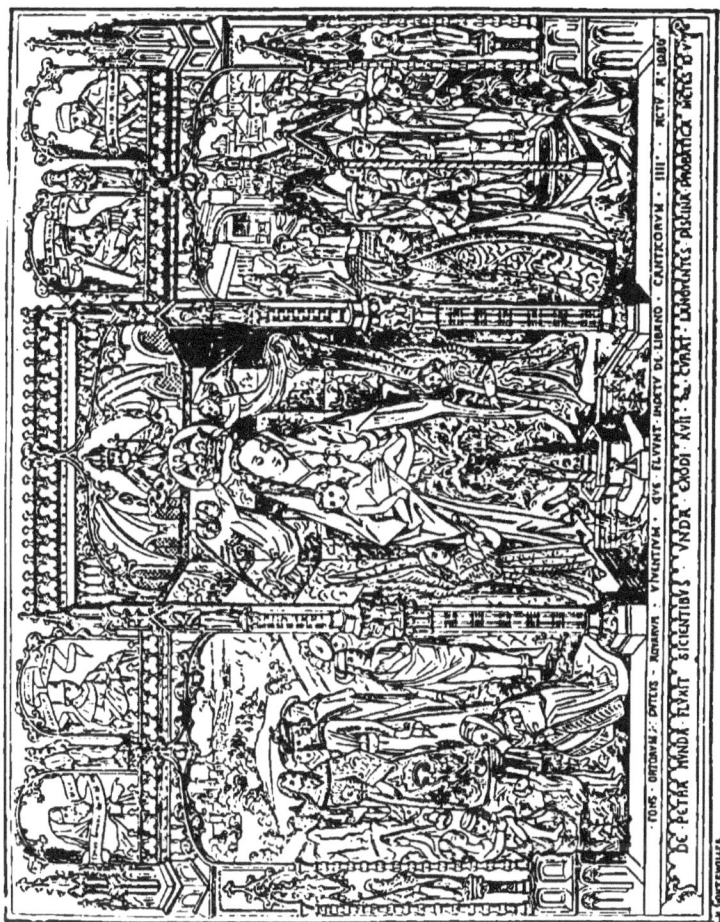

THE VIRGIN ENTHRONED. FLEMISH TAPESTRY. 1485. *The Louvre.*

To face p. 318.

have foretold. In 1484 Charles VIII. attempted to reverse the fatal policy of his predecessor, but it was too late; the industry was dead. Next in importance to Arras came Tournai, where, in 1398, regulations were made for the governance of the art. In 1423 we find that the guild was an important body in the town, and by the middle of the century the art had reached its culmination there. The fall of Arras deferred the decline of the industry at Tournai, but a pestilence which visited the town in 1513 killed half the population, and dealt a blow to the tapestry industry from which it did not recover.

A guild of tapestry weavers was chartered at Oudenarde in 1441, and soon became prosperous, whilst the art also found a convenient home at Brussels. Tapestry looms were likewise worked at Valenciennes, Lille, Bruges, Douai, Ypres, and Mons. In these towns, however, little storied tapestry was made, the chief product was of patterned stuffs for furniture. Bruges was always more of a mart for the sale of manufactured goods than actually a manufactory. At all the towns last mentioned *Sayetterie* eventually became the chief industry, and tapestry-weaving was reduced to the second rank. *Sayetterie* made great strides at Lille, which, after the fall of Arras, became the capital of that branch of the weaving industry. There the silk-weavers and the tapestry-makers belonged to separate guilds, alway quarrelling together about the boundary between their respective crafts. At last the limits of their spheres of work were decided by a town ordinance, which the studious reader may hunt up in the pages of M. Guiffrey's splendid book.

The guilds of tapestrers jealously watched over the work of their members. Thus in the year 1476 Pierre du Jardin was condemned by the municipal authorities of Lille, on the complaint of the tapestrers, to pay a fine and to make divers expiatory pilgrimages because he had used yarn in a tapestry instead of silk thread. The guild ordinances were very precise upon these and the like matters, and even influential masters did not transgress with impunity.

The existing Flemish tapestries, accessible either directly or through the medium of photography, are neither sufficient in number nor in chronological completeness to enable us to trace the artistic development of the craft of tapestry-weaving in the Low Countries. Fourteenth-century tapestries were relatively small in size and chiefly made of wool. As the workmen advanced in technical skill they set up larger looms and they used more costly materials. Occasionally we are enabled to record some definite advance, as when Michael Bernard, master-weaver of Arras, made the great tapestry of the battle of Rosebecque, which he finished in 1387. This was the largest and the most splendid storied hanging ever seen up to that time. The name of Jean Coussin of Arras is likewise known as that of an important pioneer in his craft. The tapestries woven at the end of the fourteenth and beginning of the fifteenth centuries were large and heavy. Eventually they tore asunder by their own weight, and so had to be cut up and used in smaller pieces. Technical improvements must have been introduced to meet this difficulty, for though the tapestries which date from the end of the fifteenth and beginning of the sixteenth centuries are of large dimensions, as a visitor to South Kensington Museum may see for himself, many of them have come down to us relatively little deteriorated.

The best existing collection of Flemish tapestry is at Madrid, and all its best pieces have been photographed by Laurent of that city. The Austrian Emperor possesses some fine pieces not easily accessible to the student. The Cluny Museum at Paris and the South Kensington Museum contain some large Flemish tapestries, and a handsome series is hung in the Palace of Hampton Court. The Industrial Museum at Berlin possesses, amongst other Flemish pieces, one in which the colours have hardly faded at all. Many scattered examples are recorded and photographed in Guiffrey's work above referred to. Few indeed of these remains date from the blossoming time of the art; the large majority issue from

Y

the days of decadence after the year 1500 was passed.

Not infrequently, especially at Madrid, the design of the finer tapestries is ascribed to such masters as Jan van Eyck and Roger van der Weyden, but these attributions are of course baseless. Once again it must be reasserted that in the fifteenth century an artist had to be the member of a guild, and a member of a guild might only do those kinds of work which his guild was founded to promote. A painter might not make miniatures ; therefore all the illuminated books, Grimani breviaries, and the like ascribed to Memling, Roger, or Van Eyck may be at once struck out from the list of their works. Tapestry designing would probably be part of the work of members of the tapestrers' guilds, at all events it is not mentioned as belonging to the painters' guilds, and therefore it certainly was not done by painters. In the year 1449 Bauduin de Bailleul of Arras was the best tapestry designer so far as the Duke of Burgundy and two master-weavers of Tournai knew. Roger van der Weyden, Petrus Cristus, Gerard van der Meire, and others were the famous artists then, and the Duke of Burgundy had he thought fit might have overridden the guild laws if they stood in the way of his employ-ing any of these men to design his Golden Fleece tapestries ; he did not, however, do so because the thing was not their work.

The laws of tapestry design and the laws of design in painting are at variance one with another. A tapestry must be primarily decorative, a painting primarily expressive. Tapestry has to hang on walls, not always flat, or round pavilions where it would certainly be liable to many folds. No refinements of composition, therefore, are possible in the design. Any one can imagine the effect that would be produced by a fold down the middle of the Sixtine Madonna; tapestry must be independent of any such little matter. However much folded it must look equally fine. Any design of figures then must be loosely composed; figures need patching about rather than composing at all in the pictorial sense. Moreover, no one ever looks at the wall of a room as a whole; its decoration must often be seen from close at hand, and it must look well in every light and from every point of view. All the traditions then of pictorial art have to be abandoned by the tapestry designer, and other things being equal, the best designer will be the man who keeps himself to that class of work. These differences were understood in Flanders at the blossoming time of the art, and hence came that apparently strange but really right style of design which governs the distribution of figures in the best large tapestries. There have been worse tapestries than those for which Raphael drew the cartoons, because, after all, he obeyed some of the

Y 2

laws which must always govern this kind of work. The later schools of the sixteenth, seventeenth, and eighteenth centuries produced many a far uglier hanging, and modern looms have sunk to a lower depth still in their imitations of finished paintings, ugly in colour, nasty in texture, unsuitable for use, and incapable of giving delight. Recently one artist has shown that the art need not be regarded as dead, and that if a good cartoon be drawn, workmen can be created capable of executing it; but that anything like a general revival can be looked for in these machine-grinding days is perhaps more than the most sanguine will expect.

INDEX OF ARTISTS.

INDEX OF PLACES.

Richard Clay and Sons, London and Bungay.

A LIST OF BOOKS PUBLISHED BY

SEELEY & CO.

46, 47 & 48, ESSEX STREET, STRAND, W.C.

(*LATE OF 54 FLEET STREET*).

PUBLISHERS OF THE PORTFOLIO, *an Artistic Periodical.*

Published Monthly.   Price 2s. 6d.

THE PORTFOLIO; an Artistical Periodical.   Edited
by P. G. HAMERTON.   Volume for 1886, 1*l.* 15*s.* or 2*l.* 2*s.*

Specimen of the Minor Illustrations in ' Imagination in Landscape Painting.'

IMAGINATION IN LANDSCAPE PAINTING.
By P. G. HAMERTON.   With Fourteen Copper Plates and
many Vignettes.   Price 21*s.*, cloth, gilt edges.
     Large-paper Copies (75 only), price 4*l.* 4*s.* half morocco.

THE SAÔNE: a Summer Voyage. By P. G. HAMERTON. With many Illustrations by T. Pennell. 4to. price 12s. 6d. cloth.

Large-paper Copies (250 only), price 1l. 11s. 6d.

Specimen of the Illustrations in ' The Saône.'

PICTURESQUE ARCHITECTURE. Twenty Plates by Ernest George, Lalanne, Lhermitte, &c. &c. Imp. 4to. price 21s. cloth.

CAMBRIDGE. By J. W. CLARK, M.A. With Twelve Etchings and numerous Vignettes by A. Brunet-Debaines and H. Toussaint. Price 1l. 1s.

'A thoroughly artistic work of topographical description and ill tion.'—*Illustrated London News.*

ETCHINGS IN BELGIUM. Thirty Plates. By
ERNEST GEORGE. New Edition. On hand-made paper, imperial 4to. 1*l*. 1*s*.

'A book to be loved and prized by all to whom art is dear.'—*Standard.*

TRISON ROOM ABOVE TE NORMAN TOWER

WINDSOR. By the Rev. W. J. LOFTIE. With
Twelve Plates and very numerous Vignettes. Cloth, gilt edges, price 21*s*.

Large-paper Copies, price 4*l*. 4*s*. half morocco.

THE ITCHEN VALLEY FROM TICHBORNE TO
SOUTHAMPTON. Twenty-two Etchings by HEYWOOD
SUMNER. Price 1*l.* 11*s.* 6*d.*
'We heartily commend it to artists.'—*Athenæum.*

THE AVON FROM NASEBY TO TEWKESBURY.
Twenty-one Etchings by HEYWOOD SUMNER. Price 1*l.* 11*s.* 6*d.*
Large-paper Copies, with Proofs of the Plates, 5*l.* 5*s.*
'Deserves high praise.'—*Academy.*

Specimen of the Minor Illustrations in 'Paris.'

PARIS IN OLD AND PRESENT TIMES, with
Especial Reference to Changes in its Architecture and Topo-
graphy. By P. G. HAMERTON. With Twelve Plates and
many Vignettes. Price 21*s.* cloth, gilt edges.
Large-paper Copies, price 4*l.* 4*s.* vellum.

AN ENGLISH VERSION OF THE ECLOGUES
OF VIRGIL. By the late SAMUEL PALMER. With Illustrations by the Author. Fourteen Copper-plates. Price 21*s.* cloth.

LANCASHIRE.   By LEO H. GRINDON.   With Four-
teen Etchings and numerous Vignettes.   Price 1*l.* 1*s.*   Large-'
paper Copies, with Proofs of the Plates, 3*l.* 3*s.*

'Cannot fail to delight those who admire good artistic work.'—*Liverpool Daily Post.*

Specimen of the Minor Illustrations in 'Stratford-on-Avon.'

STRATFORD-ON-AVON, from the Earliest Times to
the Death of Shakespeare.   By SIDNEY L. LEE.   With Fourteen Plates and Thirty-one Vignettes, by E. HULL.   Price 21*s.*
cloth, gilt edges.   Large-paper Copies, price 4*l.* 4*s.*, vellum.

'A really valuable and acceptable Christmas gift-book.'—*Guardian.*

MICHEL ANGELO, LIONARDO DA VINCI, AND
RAPHAEL. By CHARLES CLEMENT. With Eight Illustrations on Copper. Price 10s. 6d.

ISIS AND THAMESIS: Hours on the River from Oxford to Henley. By Professor A. J. CHURCH. With Twelve Plates and many Vignettes. Cloth, gilt edges, 16s. Also a Large-paper Edition, with Proofs of the Plates. Price 42s. half morocco.

Specimen of the Minor Illustrations in ' Isis and Thamesis.'

OXFORD. Chapters by A. LANG. With Ten Etchings by A. Brunet-Debaines, A. Toussaint, and R. Kent Thomas, and several Vignettes. Price 1l. 1s.

' Told in Mr. Lang's best style, and beautifully illustrated.'—*Literary Churchman.*

LANDSCAPE. By PHILIP GILBERT HAMERTON, Author of 'Etching and Etchers,' 'The Graphic Arts,' &c. Columbier 8vo., with Fifty Illustrations, 5l. 5s.
Large-paper Copies, with Proofs of the Engravings, 10l. 10s.

' The superb volume before us may be said to represent, so far as this country is concerned, illustration, decoration, typography, and taste in binding at their best, employed on a work devoted to the fine arts exclusively.'—*Athenæum.*

THE GRAPHIC ARTS : A Treatise on the Varieties of Drawing, Painting, and Engraving. By PHILIP GILBERT HAMERTON. With Fifty-four Illustrations.

' This massive and authorative treatise on the technical part of almost every branch of art. . . . It is the masterpiece of Mr. Hamerton. . . . A beautiful work of lasting value.'—*Saturday Review.*

THE RUINED ABBEYS OF YORKSHIRE. By
W. CHAMBERS LEFROY. With Twelve Etchings and numerous
Vignettes. Price 1*l.* 1*s.*
'A very charming volume.'—*Leeds Mercury.*

EDINBURGH. Etchings from Drawings by S. Bough,
R.S.A., and W. E. Lockhart, R.S.A. Vignettes by Hector
Chalmers. Text by ROBERT LOUIS STEVENSON. Price 18*s.*
'Altogether a very charming gift-book.'—*Pall Mall Gazette.*

Specimen of the Illustrations in 'Early Flemish Artists.'

EARLY FLEMISH ARTISTS, AND THEIR PRE-
DECESSORS ON THE LOWER RHINE. By W. M. CONWAY.
With Twenty-nine Illustrations. Price 7*s.* 6*d.* cloth.

THE ARTISTIC DEVELOPMENT OF REY-
NOLDS AND GAINSBOROUGH. By W. M. CONWAY.
With Sixteen Illustrations. Price 5*s.* cloth, gilt edges.

SCHOOLS OF MODERN ART IN GERMANY.
By J. BEAVINGTON ATKINSON. With Fifteen Etchings and numerous Woodcuts. Price 1*l.* 11*s.* 6*d.* Large-paper Copies, with Plates on India paper, price 3*l.* 3*s.*

' In every respect worthy of its subject.'—*Athenæum.*

THE ABBEY CHURCH OF ST. ALBANS. By
J. W. COMYNS CARR. Illustrated with Five Etchings by Ernest George and R. Kent Thomas, and many smaller Illustrations. Price 18*s.*

' A bright, comprehensive history of the Abbey, with beautiful etchings and many woodcuts.'

LIFE OF ALBERT DÜRER. By Mrs. CHARLES
HEATON. New Edition. With Portrait and Sixteen Illustrations. Price 10*s.* 6*d.*

' In its present form Mrs. Heaton's work deserves high commendation.'—*Guardian.*

ETCHINGS FROM THE NATIONAL GALLERY.
Eighteen Plates by Flameng, Rajon, Le Rat, &c. With Notes by R. N. WORNUM. Large 4to. 1*l.* 11*s.* 6*d.* cloth, gilt edges.

ETCHINGS FROM THE NATIONAL GALLERY.
Second Series. Eighteen Plates. Text by R. N. WORNUM. 1*l.* 11*s.* 6*d.*

EIGHTEEN ETCHINGS BY ENGLISH, FRENCH,
AND GERMAN ARTISTS. Comprising Plates by Seymour Haden, Ernest George, Brunet-Debaines, &c. With Notes by P. G. HAMERTON. Imperial 4to. 1*l.* 11*s.* 6*d.* cloth, gilt edges.

FRENCH ARTISTS OF THE PRESENT DAY.
Twelve Facsimile Engravings after Pictures. With Notices of the Painters by RENE MENARD. Large 4to. 1*l.* 1*s.* cloth, gilt edges.

' A handsome and most interesting book.'—*Times.*

FLAXMAN'S CLASSICAL OUTLINES. Cheap
Edition for the use of Schools of Designs. With Notes by J. C. L. SPARKES, Head Master of the National Art Training Schools, South Kensington. 14*s.* complete, cloth.

THE SYLVAN YEAR: Leaves from the Note-Book
of Raoul Dubois. By P. G. HAMERTON. With Twenty Etchings, by the Author and other Artists. 8vo. 12*s.* 6*d.* cloth. Cheap Edition, with Eight Etchings. Price 5*s.*

CHAPTERS ON ANIMALS. By P. G. HAMERTON.
With Twenty Etchings. Post 8vo. 12*s.* 6*d.* cloth. Cheap Edition, with Eight Etchings. Price 5*s.*

A CANTERBURY PILGRIMAGE. Ridden, Written, and Illustrated by JOSEPH & ELIZABETH PENNELL. Price 1s.; cloth, gilt edges, 2s. 6d.

'The most wonderful shillingsworth that modern literature has to offer.'
Daily News.

AN ITALIAN PILGRIMAGE. By Mrs. PENNELL. With many Illustrations by J. Pennell. Price 6s. cloth.

Specimen of the Illustrations in 'An Italian Pilgrimage.'

FLATLAND : A Romance of Many Dimensions. By A. SQUARE. Price 2s. 6d.

'This book is at once a popular scientific treatise of great value, and a fairy tale worthy to rank with "The Water Babies" and "Alice in Wonderland."'—*Oxford Magazine.*

SINTRAM AND HIS COMPANIONS. By DE LA MOTTE FOUQUE. A New Translation. With numerous Illustrations by Heywood Sumner. Cloth, price 5s.

JAMES HANNINGTON. First Bishop of Eastern
Equatorial Africa. A Memoir. By the Rev. E. C. DAWSON,
M.A. With Portrait, and Illustrations after the Bishop's own
Sketches. Price 7s. 6d. cloth.

FOREST OUTLAWS; OR, ST. HUGH AND THE
KING. By the Rev. E. GILLIAT. With Sixteen Illustrations.
Price 5s. cloth.

HORACE WALPOLE AND HIS WORLD. Select
passages from his Letters. With Eight copper-plates after Sir
Joshua Reynolds and Sir Thomas Lawrence. Cloth, price 6s.
Also a Large-paper Edition, with Proofs of the Plates, price
12s. 6d.

FATHER ALDUR: a Water Story. By A. GIBERNE.
With Sixteen Tinted Illustrations. Price 5s. cloth.

AMONG THE STARS; OR, WONDERFUL THINGS
IN THE SKY. By A. GIBERNE. With Illustrations. *Third*
Thousand. Price 5s.

SUN, MOON, AND STARS. A Book on Astronomy
for Beginners. By A. GIBERNE. With Coloured Illustrations.
Twelfth Thousand. Cloth, price 5s.

'Ought to have a place in village libraries and mechanics' institutions;
would also be welcome as a prize-book.'—*Pall Mall Gazette.*

THE WORLD'S FOUNDATIONS. Geology for
Beginners. By A. GIBERNE. With Illustrations. *Third*
Thousand. Cloth, price 5s.

'The exposition is clear, the style simple and attractive.'—*Spectator.*

MODERN FRENCHMEN. Five Biographies. By
P. G. HAMERTON. Post 8vo. 7s. 6d. cloth.

I. VICTOR JACQUEMONT.	III. FRANCOIS RUDE.
II. HENRY PERREYVE.	IV. JEAN JACQUES AMPERE.

V. HENRI REGNAULT.

ROUND MY HOUSE. Notes of Rural Life in France
in Peace and War. *Third Edition.* 5s. cloth.

A SHORT HISTORY OF NAPOLEON THE
FIRST. By Professor SEELEY. With Portrait. Price 5s. cloth.
'Within the limits which the author has set himself the essay seems
to us one of singular force and brilliancy.'—*Guardian.*

STORIES OF THE MAGICIANS. By Professor
A. J. CHURCH. With Coloured Illustrations. Price 5*s.* cloth.

WITH THE KING AT OXFORD. By Professor
A. J. CHURCH. With Coloured Illustrations. Price 5*s.* cloth.

THE CHANTRY PRIEST OF BARNET: a Tale
of the Two Roses. By Professor A. J. CHURCH. With Coloured Illustrations, price 5*s.*

STORIES FROM THE CLASSICS. By the Rev.
A. J. CHURCH, M.A., Professor of Latin at University College,
London. With Coloured Illustrations.

STORIES FROM HOMER. 5*s.*
STORIES FROM VIRGIL. 5*s.*
STORIES FROM THE GREEK TRAGEDIANS. 5*s.*
STORIES OF THE EAST FROM HERODOTUS. 5*s.*
THE STORY OF THE PERSIAN WAR. 5*s.*
STORIES FROM LIVY. 5*s.*
ROMAN LIFE IN THE DAYS OF CICERO. 5*s.*
THE STORY OF THE LAST DAYS OF JERUSALEM.
3*s.* 6*d.*
A TRAVELLER'S TRUE TALE FROM LUCIAN. 3*s.* 6*d.*
HEROES AND KINGS. 1*s.* 6*d.*

BORDER LANCES. By the Author of 'Belt and
Spur.' With Coloured Illustrations. Price 5*s.*

BELT AND SPUR. Stories of the Knights of Old.
By the same Author. *Third Thousand.* With Sixteen Illumi-
nations. Cloth, price 5*s.*
'A sort of boys' Froissart, with admirable illustrations.'—*Pall Mall
Gazette.*

THE CITY IN THE SEA. Stories of the Old
Venetians. By the Author of 'Belt and Spur.' With Coloured
Illustrations. Cloth, price 5*s.*

STORIES OF THE ITALIAN ARTISTS FROM
VASARI. By the Author of 'Belt and Spur.' With Coloured
Illustrations, price 5*s.* cloth.

THE PHARAOHS AND THEIR LAND: Scenes of
Old Egyptian Life and History. By E. BERKLEY. With
Coloured Illustrations. Cloth, price 5*s.*
'An account of that wonderful land which is not only interesting, but
valuable.'—*Leeds Mercury.*

Specimen of the Illustrations in 'Stories of the Italian Painters.'

SUE; OR, WOUNDED IN SPORT. By E. VINCENT
BRITON, Author of 'Amyot Brough.' Price 1s. sewed; 1s. 6d.
cloth.

'Shows both pathos and humour. Sue and her lover Abner are fine
figures, and the easy Monroe household is a forcibly satirical sketch.'
Pall Mall Gazette.

AMYOT BROUGH. By E. VINCENT BRITON. With
Illustrations. Price 5s. cloth.

'With national pride we dwell on a beautiful English historical novel
. . . this sweet unpretending story, with its pretty engravings.'—*Academy.*

THE TOWER ON THE CLIFF: a Legend. By
EMMA MARSHALL, Author of 'Under the Mendips,' &c.
Price 1s. sewed; 1s. 6d. cloth.

'Founded on an old legend attaching to a Gloucestershire castle,
which has afforded the authoress material for working up a romantic
story.'—*Times.*

Specimen of the Illustrations in 'Australia.'

AUSTRALIA; OR, ENGLAND IN THE SOUTH. By
G. SUTHERLAND, M.A., of Melbourne University. With
Illustrations. Price 1s. sewed; 1s. 6d. cloth.

'A very interesting and instructive little work.'—*Times.*

CHAPTERS ON FLOWERS. By CHARLOTTE
ELIZABETH. A New Edition, with Coloured Illustrations.
Price 5s. cloth.

www.ingramcontent.com/pod-product-compliance
Lightning Source LLC
Chambersburg PA
CBHW021109270326
41929CB00009B/793